THE FALCON WARE STORY

The History and Products of

J.H. WEATHERBY & SONS LTD
FALCON POTTERY
OLD TOWN ROAD
HANLEY
STOKE-ON-TRENT

THOMAS LAWRENCE (LONGTON) LTD
FALCON WORKS
LONGTON
STOKE-ON-TRENT

FALCON CHINA LTD
HEATHS PASSAGE
WARREN STREET
LONGTON
STOKE-ON-TRENT

ACKNOWLEDGEMENTS

It would be impossible to compile a reference book such as this without help from many people. An important part of the information has been provided by collectors from all over the World, it has been rather like having many research assistants constantly searching for vital information.

Thank you: Barry Broadhurst, Jean Brookes, Malcolm Chapman, Jackie and Tony Chew, Harold Clowes, Sheila Cox, Fabienne Daniel, Lewis Dunkley, Lance Edwards, Grace Finch, Dorothy Gallagher, Geoff Gibbon, Jane Hallsworth, Marie Hammond, Sandra Hancock, Jean and Peter Howard, Helen Jamieson, Jackie Kaldenberg, Glennys Leatherbarrow, Geoff Lynch, Shona McNeill, Anne Morgan, Penny Morgan, John Paley, Lesley and Mike Pardoe, Jayne and David Richards, Shirley and Jim Robson, Steve Rumsey, Jean Simms, Brian Stalley, Margaret and John Stiles, E. Roy Taylor, Penny Teerman, Pauline and John Thake, Denise and Paul Tripp, Barbara Turner, Janice and Terry Waller, Rosemary Woolger, for providing information and photographs. Apologies for any names inadvertently omitted from this list.

I am indebted to Jeanette Holdcroft, daughter of Mr. Reginald Thompson, for the loan of important documents and photographs. Peter Landon for local research, Portmeirion Potteries Ltd., for access to information, Clive J. Hillier at Louis Taylor for the auction information, Mr. & Mrs. Brian Winstanley and Mrs. K. Parker for donating the Grundy photographs, Angela Lee at the Gladstone Pottery Museum for access to records, and Mick and Derry Collins for the loan of photographs, and documents.

We met Malcolm Harris during the book launch of The SylvaC Story in 1989, when he attended all three days of events in Stoke-on-Trent. He was a very enthusiastic researcher and collector, who constantly supplied new information. Despite failing health he was very interested in this latest project, The Falcon Ware Story, providing photographs and newspaper cuttings until just a few weeks before he died in November 1995. Our condolences go to his wife Elaine, who kindly gave us permission to use Malcolm's photographs.

Illustrations from the Pottery Gazette by courtesy of Tableware International. Photographs and articles reproduced from the Evening Sentinel by kind permission of Sentinel Newspapers Ltd., Stoke-on-Trent.

Thanks to: Mr. & Mrs. Stuart Weatherby, Mrs. Edna Weatherby, Mr. Christopher Weatherby and Mr. Jonathan Weatherby, for their friendly hospitality, access to, and use of family and factory documents, Mr. Ivan Dean for his helpful co-operation with this project.

My husband, Peter, has been a constant support to me throughout the research, compilation and publication procedures for which I am very grateful.

Although every care has been taken to eliminate errors, the possibility always exists. Readers who have noticed any mistakes or who have additional information to offer are invited to contact the author at Pottery Publications. Additional copies of this book may be purchased from Pottery Publications.

Published by Pottery Publications, 7 Merton Park Parade, Kingston Road, London SW19 3NT.
Phototypeset by Intype, Woodman Works, Durnsford Road, London SW19 8DR.
Printed by Biddles Limited, Woodbridge Park Estate, Woodbridge Road, Guildford, Surrey GU1 1DA.

First Edition 1996 ISBN 0 9514889 3 7

CONTENTS

INTRODUCTION

The Falcon Ware Story features three quite different potteries, all from the Stoke-on-Trent area. They have no connection with each other apart from the Falcon name. There is often confusion as to the origins of Falcon Ware, and it is hoped The Falcon Ware Story will clarify this.

PART ONE is about J.H. Weatherby & Sons Ltd, Falcon Pottery, Hanley, this company was founded in 1891 by Mr. J.H. Weatherby, is still producing wares, and has Mr. Christopher Weatherby the great grandson of the founder at the helm. It is a company specialising in hotel and gift ware, with a few interesting diversions in the 1950's and 1960's.

PART TWO tells a different tale of another family run pottery. Thomas Lawrence (Longton) Ltd., Falcon Pottery, Longton, was formed c1888 by Mr. Thomas Lawrence, this passed into the hands of his nephew Mr. John Grundy then Mr. Grundy's son-in-law Mr. Richard Hull, and eventually finished trading in 1962. Their range consisted of utility and fancy ware with particularly stylish decorations.

PART THREE features a more recently formed pottery, also a family run business, Falcon China, Longton, specialising in the production of trinket boxes. This company was formed in 1990 by Mr. Ivan Dean with the help of his family, who run a comparatively small but successful business.

PART ONE

J.H. Weatherby & Sons,
LIMITED
TRADE
MARK
DURABILITY
J.H.W & SONS,
HANLEY,
ENGLAND.
FALCON WARE
MANUFACTURERS OF
Earthenware.
Falcon Pottery,
HANLEY,
Staffordshire, England.

PREFACE TO PART ONE

The blame for writing this book can be laid squarely on the shoulders of dealer/collector Geoff Lynch, from Bournemouth, who introduced us to the delights of the Weatherby Zookies. As any collector knows, once an interest has been sparked all hope is lost, and it wasn't long before we became fully fledged Weatherby collectors.

Not only were we on the look out for Zookies, Life Like animals, Beasties and Sea Twinks, but we had succumbed to the pre-war delights of the 1930s, the Art Deco period, and even earlier. The inevitable trail led to the J.H. Weatherby & Sons Ltd, Falcon Pottery, and it was with considerable surprise we found they were still functioning as a family concern, and even had several Mr. Weatherbys' in management.

We were hopeful that as the business had been passed from father to sons, to grandsons, and now to great grandson, there would be considerable archival material available, and we were not disappointed.

It was an absolute joy to find that Mr. J. Lucas Weatherby, the founder's grandson, was helpful and co-operative, he took us on a tour of the factory explaining all the various processes to us. He had a formidable knowledge of each department, having dedicated all his working life to the success of the family business.

Sadly Mr. J. Lucas Weatherby passed away suddenly on 6th May 1993. Mr. Christopher Weatherby, took his place at the helm, and it was at his suggestion we contacted his father Mr. J. Stuart Weatherby, former joint managing director, who kindly allowed us to borrow family and business papers in order that we could complete this project. Mrs. Edna Weatherby, widow of Mr. J. Lucas Weatherby very kindly lent many of the documents, press cuttings and family photographs in her possession. Mr. Christopher Weatherby and Mr. Jonathan Weatherby (sales director) have given us every possible assistance and allowed us unrestricted access to the company archives.

May we take this opportunity to thank all the Weatherby family for their kindness and assistance, and for sparing us so much of their valuable time. They have a fine collection of Weatherby Ware and we have referred to these items as the 'Weatherby Collection'.

CHAPTER ONE
HISTORY OF THE COMPANY

J.H. Weatherby & Sons Ltd
Falcon Pottery
Hanley
Stoke-on-Trent

In 1726 John Weatherby, a potter, left Woodhead, near Bagnall, in the parish of Burslem, Stoke-on-Trent, to become a potter and glassmaker in London. By 1750 he was part owner of the Bow Pottery, he died in 1758. Every generation of the Weatherby family since then has produced at least one person connected with the pottery industry, and our story begins with Henry Weatherby, the father of the founder of J.H. Weatherby & Sons Ltd.

Henry Weatherby, born in 1818, was a potter's turner, living in Stoke-on-Trent. He married Ann Clews in 1838, and three children were born, Rachel in 1839, Jane in 1841 and John Henry in 1843. Tragedy struck in 1845, when Henry died from pneumonia at the age of 27. This was directly as a result of his heroism in rescuing a drowning child from one of the canal locks at Longport. His widow, Ann Weatherby, died in 1885.

Thus, John Henry Weatherby, born in 1843, fatherless from the age of two, eventually became apprenticed to his uncle, William Wood, of Wood and Company, Albert Street in Burslem, where amongst other skills learned he became a thrower and turner. He married Mary Mawdesley in 1864, they had two sons Samuel Mawdesley and John Henry junior, and two daughters Mary and Jane Ann. In 1882, after many years of experience in most aspects of the pottery business, he left his uncles employment and became a third partner in the firm of Whittaker, Edge & Co., Hallfield Pottery, Festing Street, Hanley, which is situated behind the existing premises of Weatherby.

When this partnership was dissolved in 1891, it seemed an opportune time to fulfill his ambition of owning his own factory, and he bought land which formed part of the Shelton Hall Estate in Shelton near Hanley, with this in mind. However this ambition was not realised due to objections by local residents who were concerned about the possibility of smoke nuisance, and the land was eventually sold back to Hanley Corporation.

John Henry senior then decided to lease an already established factory, Pinnox Works in Pinnox Street, Tunstall, and with great enthusiasm, and supported and encouraged by his two sons he started the firm of J.H. Weatherby & Sons. We think part of the original Pinnox Works still exists, and is now used by an engineering business called Pinnox Metal Works.

However all was not well at the Tunstall factory. The leasing agreement entered into, whereby the factory had to be maintained and kept in good order, meant that much of the profit was taken to keep the factory buildings up to standard. Another problem also came to light soon after opening the factory. John Henry senior had estimated his works costs and selling prices on the same basis as the Hanley factory. He had not realised the Tunstall workers required higher wages for making and decorating the same wares. This venture was clearly going to be unprofitable, and they decided to close the factory, but were bound by the lease he had signed. After one year, with the help of lawyers, and having to pay compensation to the factory owners, John Henry, was released from the contract. (Incidentally, the family lawyer was the father of the author Arnold Bennett).

During the first year a distinctive Union Jack logo was designed and is still in use to-day. The Tunstall name was incorporated into the mark, from which one immediately identifies the piece as being an early Weatherby product. It is thought toilet sets, table ware and utility items were probably produced at this time.

John Henry senior was resigned to returning to his former employment after leaving Tunstall, but with the support of his family who rallied round, they found other premises in Hanley, the Falcon Pottery in the High Street, (now Old Town Road). The cost of this move had taken most of his available capital so they sold all the ware they could from Tunstall, and transported the remaining equipment on wagons to Hanley. The family loaded the wagons themselves in order to save money. On September 27th 1892 a circular letter was sent to all their customers advising them of the new address.

The Falcon Pottery had been unoccupied for some time, consequently the bottle ovens were damp and required three firings before a satisfactory piece of biscuit ware was glazed. They soon overcame these initial difficulties, and the first Weatherby ware manufactured at the Falcon Pottery was underway.

The Falcon Pottery was formed from several factories and the works were previously known as Gelson Works and Cobden Works, parts of which date back to 1779. On December 1st 1906 the following article appeared in the Pottery Gazette, and we reproduce this in full for your interest:

'J.H. Weatherby & Sons, earthenware manufacturers, of the Falcon Pottery, High Street, Hanley, have recently been making extensive alterations and additions to their works, which are now almost completed. The old offices of the firm have been cleared away in order to make room for a commodious and substantial three-storey building, which, on the two upper floors, gives extensive new warehouse and showroom accommodation, while on the ground floor a handsome suite of offices is being installed. The show or sample-room on the second floor is a feature which will be greatly appreciated by the firm's customers, who will be able to select their goods more conveniently than they did formerly, when it was necessary for them to walk through a large area of the works in order to make their choice. The extensions which have taken place are primarily due to the appreciation the trade and public have evinced for Messrs. Weatherby's productions, which certainly hold a high place for quality, value and durability. Their trade mark is the English flag with the word "Durability" stamped across it, and it is the constant endeavour of the firm to "live up" to their trade mark. For fifteen years the business has been constantly growing, and recently they had to increase their plant again in order to cope with the demands made upon them. All classes of dinner ware, tea, toilet, and fancy wares are produced for the home, foreign and Colonial markets alike, and in all grades, both plain and decorated. One of the latest productions is an attractive suite of jugs, teapots, salads, &c., called the "Royal Pansy" pottery, which is very prettily decorated with pansies. The new warehouse accommodation now provided will enable the firm to execute orders more quickly than has been the case in the past, and will facilitate and expedite business in many ways.'

It would appear from the above article that J.H. Weatherby & Sons were already expanding and updating the business in 1906, in 1908 they became a limited company. The business still continues successfully to-day (1996) in the hands of the great grandsons of the founder. It is quite rare to find an independent family run business in the pottery industry, and it is to be hoped they will carry on for many years to come.

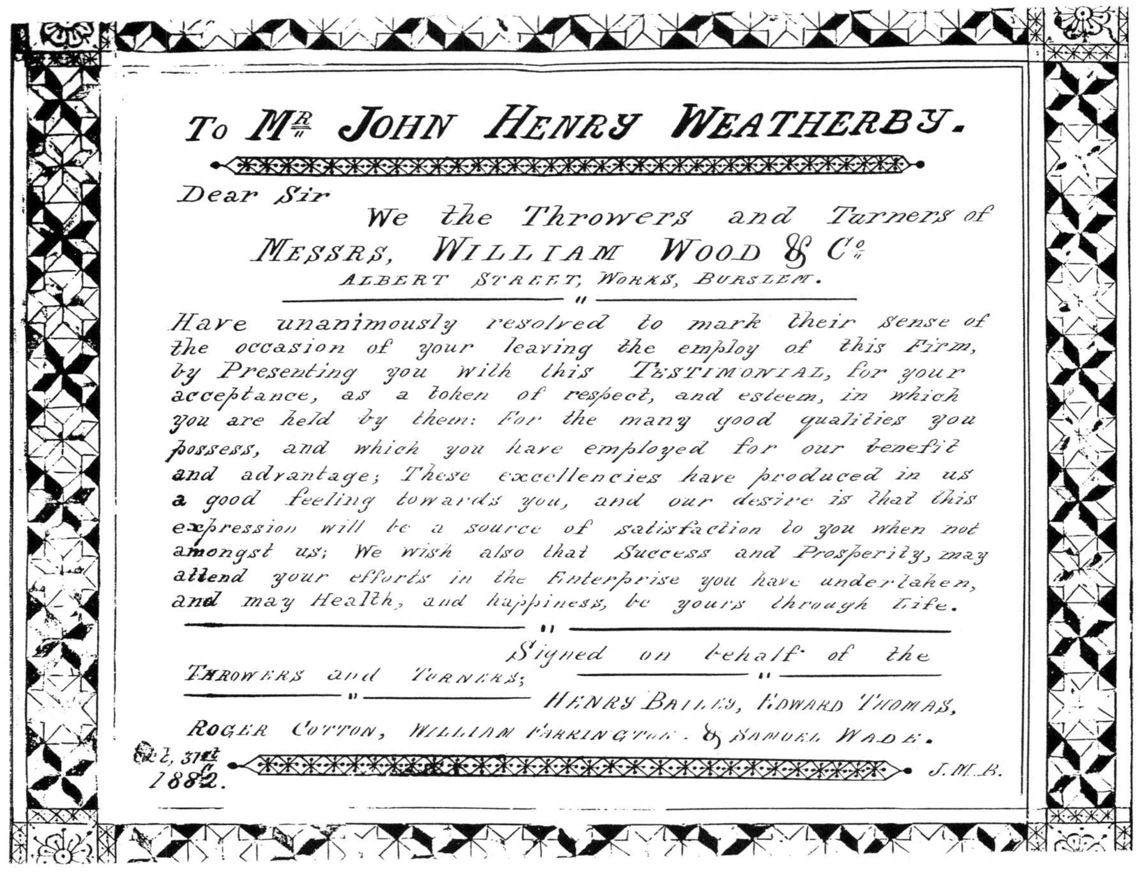

To Mr. John Henry Weatherby.

Dear Sir

We the Throwers and Turners of Messrs, William Wood & Co.
Albert Street, Works, Burslem.

Have unanimously resolved to mark their sense of the occasion of your leaving the employ of this Firm, by Presenting you with this Testimonial, for your acceptance, as a token of respect, and esteem, in which you are held by them: For the many good qualities you possess, and which you have employed for our benefit and advantage; These excellencies have produced in us a good feeling towards you, and our desire is that this expression will be a source of satisfaction to you when not amongst us; We wish also that Success and Prosperity, may attend your efforts in the Enterprise you have undertaken, and may Health, and happiness, be yours through Life.

Signed on behalf of the Throwers and Turners;
Henry Bailey, Edward Thomas, Roger Cotton, William Farrington & Samuel Wade.

Oct. 31st 1882.

J.M.B.

▲ Testimonial presented to Mr. J.H. Weatherby senior on the occasion of his leaving the employment of William Wood & Co., dated October 31st 1882.

▼ In 1882 Mr. J.H. Weatherby senior took a third partnership in the firm of Whittaker, Edge & Co., Hallfield Pottery, Festing Street, Hanley. This photograph of Hallfield Pottery was taken in 1994.

TELEGRAPHIC ADDRESS:
"WEATHERBY,"
TUNSTALL.

TELEPHONE, No. 537.

Pinnox Works,
Tunstall, Staffs.

Aug. 20th, 1891.

Dear Sir,

You will doubtless have learned of the dissolution of my late firm of Whittaker & Co., and I have pleasure in informing you that I have taken the "Pinnox Works, Tunstall," formerly in the occupation of Messrs. Wedgwood & Co.

A similar class of business will be carried on at the above Works under the style of "J. H. Weatherby & Sons," and having ample accomodation, with the most recent improvements in Machinery, etc. It will be our aim to produce the best goods in Plain, Printed and Decorated Earthenware, for Home and Export trade.

Not the least advantage that we shall possess will be the valuable services of the Artist (Mr. Stanway), who has so successfully designed the new patterns for the late firm, and you can therefore confidently rely on the newest and best shapes and designs being introduced.

Thanking you personally for the favours bestowed on W. and Co., and hoping that by strict attention and promptitude, to participate in your future orders.

I remain, Yours obediently,

J. H. Weatherby, trading as

J. H. WEATHERBY & SONS.

Printed by Atkinson Brothers, *Hanley*

◄ In 1891, Mr. J.H. Weatherby senior left Whittaker, Edge & Co., and together with his sons Samuel and John junior started his own company at the Pinnox Works, Pinnox Street, Tunstall. A letter was sent to prospective clients, dated Aug. 20th, 1891, informing them of this fact.

► Photograph taken in 1994, showing portion of the Pinnox Works, Pinnox Street, still standing, now called Pinnox Metal Works. The rest of the works has been demolished.

TELEGRAPHIC ADDRESS:
"WEATHERBY, HANLEY."

TELEPHONE NO. 97

Hanley, Staffs.,

September 27th, 1892.

Dear Sir,

E respectfully beg to inform you that we have removed from Tunstall to the

FALCON POTTERY, HIGH STREET, HANLEY,

STAFFS.,

where we shall continue to carry on the Manufacture of

GENERAL EARTHENWARE

(PRINTED & DECORATED)

suitable for the Home and Foreign Markets, and hope by giving personal attention to the prompt and careful execution of all Orders, to be favoured with a continuance of your esteemed commands. Thanking you for past favours,

We remain,

Yours obediently,

J. H. Weatherby & Sons.

Please note New Address—
FALCON POTTERY,
HANLEY.

HUGHES & HARBER, PRINTERS, LONGTON.

◀ On September 27th 1892, J.H. Weatherby & Sons moved from Tunstall to the Falcon Pottery, High Street, Hanley. This is the circular letter sent to customers.

On 29th April 1955, High Street became Town Road, and on 8th December 1986, Town Road became Old Town Road.

▼ The Falcon Pottery, Hanley, photograph taken 1986.

CHAPTER TWO
THE WEATHERBY FAMILY

A brief summary of the Weatherby family 1843–1996

MR. JOHN HENRY WEATHERBY SENIOR

Mr. John Henry Weatherby senior was born in 1843, and married Mary Mawdesley in 1864, his sons Samuel Mawdesley and John Weatherby junior were born in 1866 and 1869 respectively, there were also two daughters, Mary and Jane Ann. There were great celebrations in 1924 when Mr. & Mrs. J.H. Weatherby reached their Diamond Wedding Anniversary, this was marked by a 'Tea and Social Evening' held at the Princes Hall, Burslem, where family and friends entertained the guests. A very impressive illuminated address was presented to them by employees, and this was reproduced on Christmas cards later in the year. The original illuminated address still hangs in an office at the Falcon Pottery. Mr. & Mrs. Weatherby were eventually to celebrate their 65th anniversary five years later.

Mrs. Mary Weatherby died in November 1929, having contributed an enormous amount of practical support to her husband over many years. Mr. J.H. Weatherby senior passed away on April 30th 1933 at the age of 90. Throughout his life he had been a prominent member of the Wesley Place Methodist Church combining his love of music with choir duties, and accompanied the Tonic Sol-fa Choir when they competed in an all England competition at Crystal Palace in April 1881. Mr. Weatherby was involved in many activities, these included a directorship of Kidsgrove Gaslight Company and Burslem Star Building Society, a particular interest in the Primrose league, and he was also a 'Guardian of the Poor'.

In 1910, Mr. J.H. Weatherby designed and built a lovely family house in the heart of Alsager, which is still occupied by a member of the Weatherby family. It contains original fixtures and fittings and is virtually unchanged.

He retired from the company in 1914, leaving it in the capable hands of his sons. He spent all his working life in the pottery industry, the last 23 years at J.H. Weatherby & Sons.

At his death John Henry Weatherby senior was described as the oldest master potter in the country. A master potter being one who started on the bench actually working and 'throwing' and finishing up as a master of his craft. The original throwing wheel used by him, is still on the factory premises, a fitting memorial to the many years he spent in and associated with the pottery industry.

MR. SAMUEL MAWDESLEY WEATHERBY

Mr. Samuel Mawdesley Weatherby elder son of Mr. J.H. Weatherby senior was born in 1866, he married Annie Gertrude Salt, they had one son John Stuart. On leaving school he joined an ironmongers business, then became a dispenser in a chemist's shop in Crewe, eventually obtaining a manager's position in Cleethorpes. His knowledge of chemistry and colour manufacture, together with management skills, a particular interest in machinery, and the practical running of a business, made him an ideal partner.

He was responsible for the finances and overseeing the management of the factory, from the clay arriving and going through its various processes until it reached the glost warehouse. At that time the factory made its own colour and glazes and Samuel was responsible for the production and personally supervised the mixing.

Like his father before him, he was a dedicated member of the Wesley Place Methodist Church in Alsager. In his younger days he sang in the choir and then became organist, a position he held for 22 years, he was also a trustee of the church for 30 years, and the Trust treasurer. He passed away at the age of 72, on October 30th 1938, having been associated with the Falcon Pottery for 47 years, and eventually holding the position of senior director.

MR. JOHN HENRY WEATHERBY JUNIOR

Mr. John Henry Weatherby junior younger son of Mr. J.H. Weatherby senior, was born in 1869, he married Florence Gertrude Lucas, they had a daughter Florence Mary and a son John Lucas. He worked with his father at the Whittaker, Edge, Hallfield Pottery, gaining particular experience with the finished product. On joining the J.H. Weatherby & Sons partnership he acted as traveller and sales representative. They had stock rooms in London and most of the principal cities in England. John Henry junior would spend a week in one town, packing up samples and sending them by train to the next town on the friday night. He would then return home for the weekend, travelling on monday morning to set up samples for the next week's business. He eventually became responsible for sales and marketing.

He was closely connected with Wesley Place Methodist Church in Alsager, where he filled every position open to a layman. Among offices he held were those of Circuit Steward, Sunday School Superintendant and Trustee. John Henry junior became chairman of directors of J.H. Weatherby & Sons Ltd, and attended the factory every working day until the age of 82. He passed away in September 1954 at the age of 85, having been associated with the Falcon Pottery for 63 years.

MR. JOHN STUART WEATHERBY

Mr. John Stuart Weatherby, son of Mr. S.M. Weatherby, grandson of Mr. J.H. Weatherby senior, married Yvonne Gundry, they have three sons Christopher, John David and Jonathan, eleven grandchildren and one great-grandson, Thomas. John Stuart joined the company in 1924, and was personally tutored by his father, in all aspects of the pottery business, starting in the slip house, and eventually taking charge of all the decorators.

During the mid-1930's the Earthenware Manufacturers Association was founded to protect the price structures of the manufacturers, and he was elected to represent the company at the committee meetings of this new association. He was therefore moved away from other duties and attended to correspondence connected with prices and quotations. The untimely death of his father, Mr. S.M. Weatherby, in 1938, meant he took over some of the office and financial side of the business, the practical side his father had dealt with was taken over by Mr. John Lucas Weatherby, his cousin.

Sadly in 1991 he became partially sighted and in 1992, registered blind he retired from the firm. He has dictated many tapes about family and company history which have been transcribed by his cousin-in-law Mrs. Edna Weatherby. We have met Mr. & Mrs. John Stuart Weatherby many times in the course of researching this book, and their hospitality, and help have been much appreciated. John Stuart, in company with all the Weatherby family, made a remarkable contribution to the success of the business, due no doubt, in part, to the thorough grounding given by his father in all departments of the factory. He became a director of the company in 1938, and went on to become chairman of the company and joint managing director.

John Stuart is still associated with the Wesley Place Methodist Church, as his father and grandfather before him. He worked at J.H. Weatherby and Sons Ltd for 68 years, and is the longest serving member of the Weatherby family. He has relished every moment spent at the works, and is immensely proud of the reputation of the company.

MR. JOHN LUCAS WEATHERBY

Mr. John Lucas Weatherby was the son of Mr. J.H. Weatherby junior and grandson of Mr. J.H. Weatherby senior, and married Edna Cadman, they have one daughter Celia Mary, and a grand daughter Harriet. He joined the firm in 1930, and was trained by Mr. S.M. Weatherby, his uncle, in the same manner as his cousin. He followed in John Stuart's footsteps, gradually taking over full responsibility for various departments. In 1937 he took over travelling in the North East and continued to increase trade in that area.

He joined the RAF in 1941, and returned to J.H. Weatherby & Sons Ltd., on the cessation of hostilities in 1945, when he was made a director of the company. On his return from active service he investigated the possibility of modernising the factory. He gradually replaced the bottle ovens with either gas or electric kilns, and installed electric motors on all the machinery, replacing the original rope drive.

We met Mr. John Lucas twice during our trips to Hanley, and the second time he took us to his home, the Weatherby home his grandfather had built in Alsager, and which has been home to four generations of the Weatherby family. Unfortunately he passed away suddenly on 6th May 1993, but during the time we knew him we found him the most delightful and helpful of gentlemen, he offered us his full co-operation. Having since returned to meet his widow, Mrs. Edna Weatherby and her daughter Celia, they too, have continued to give us their full support.

Off duty his main interests were the Wesley Place Methodist Church, where he held office for over sixty years, the Nantwich and Border Counties Yacht Club, of which he was Commodore and Life President, and the St. John Ambulance Brigade. One of the highlights of his life was being admitted as an Officer (Brother) of The Order of St. John on 21st May 1980. There was an investiture at The Grand Priory Church, St. John's Square, London EC1, which was carried out by the Lord Prior on behalf of Her Majesty the Queen.

John Lucas became joint managing director and was associated with the company for 63 years. He worked at the factory until his untimely death in 1993. In common with all the other directors he shared a complete dedication to the family firm.

MR. CHRISTOPHER WEATHERBY

Mr. Christopher Weatherby is the son of Mr. J.S. Weatherby and grandson of Mr. S.M. Weatherby. He joined the company in 1972 bringing with him ten years of business experience gained from advising many companies on the use of their computer equipment. He has worked in all departments of the company and is now chairman and managing director. He is also chairman of Dalehall Mills Ltd., who supply body materials to the industry. He holds office at Wesley Place Methodist Church, continuing the long family association.

MR. JONATHAN RICHARD WEATHERBY

Mr. Jonathan Richard Weatherby is the son of Mr. J.S. Weatherby and grandson of Mr. S.M. Weatherby, he joined the company in 1970 starting on the clay production side. He then went on to decorating and dispatch and sales. He is now sales director, involved in home and overseas sales.

SHARE HOLDERS

Share holders in the company are Mr. C.S. Weatherby, Mr. J.R. Weatherby, Mrs. Edna Weatherby, Mr. John David Harvey Weatherby son of Mr. J.S. Weatherby, and Mrs. Celia Mary Crompton née Weatherby, daughter of Mr. J.L. Weatherby.

◄ Mr. S.M. Weatherby and Mr. J.H. Weatherby junior (sons of the founder) in their office at Falcon Works.

▲ Mr. S.M. Weatherby, Mr. J.H. Weatherby, Mr. J.H. Weatherby junior, a photograph taken c1910.

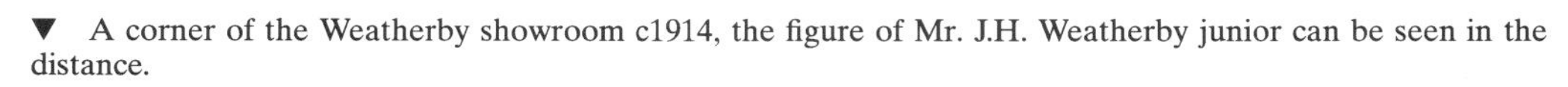

▼ A corner of the Weatherby showroom c1914, the figure of Mr. J.H. Weatherby junior can be seen in the distance.

▲ Weatherby display set up in an hotel room, which was the custom at the time (pre 1914). A different town was visited each week, and prospective customers would be invited to inspect the wares and place their orders.

◀ A card was hung on the door of the hotel room where the Weatherby goods were displayed. Mr. A.S. Parkyn was the representative who took the orders on this occasion.

▲ Mr. & Mrs. J.H. Weatherby senior on the porch of the house they designed and had built in 1910. Their two daughters are seated in the Model T Ford car. Miss Mary Weatherby is in the driving seat, beside her is her husband to be Mr. E. Millward. Seated at the back is Miss Jane Weatherby. c1922.

▶ Photograph taken in 1994 of the same house, with Mrs. E. Weatherby, who still resides at the house, and her daughter Mrs. C. Crompton. The porch has been filled in, but otherwise the house looks remarkably unchanged.

1864 1924

To Mr. & Mrs. J. H. Weatherby.

Parkholme, Alsager.

The Employees of Messrs. J. H. Weatherby & Sons. Ltd., take this opportunity of offering you their sincerest congratulations on the occasion of Your Diamond Wedding and, in commemoration of such a happy event, ask your acceptance of this Illuminated Address.

Whilst offering you their hearty felicitations, they would like to place on record the good feeling which has always existed between yourselves and the Employees for the past 30 years, and desire to show their appreciation of your impartial manner and kindly thoughts, which have always gained their respect and esteem.

It is their earnest wish that Divine Providence may continue to watch over you and yours, and that you may both be spared for many years to come to continue your association with them.

Signed on behalf of the Employees:-

G. Cadman, Chairman. W. Smith, D. Johnson,
T. Broome, J. Hughes, Mrs. M. H. Austin,
J. C. Wilkinson, J. Woodward, Mrs. E. Ellis,
H. Slater, J. Ellis, Mrs. M. Sawyer,
E. Curzon, F. Clough, Miss H. Stevenson.

Falcon Pottery,
High Street, Hanley.
April 2nd. 1924.

◀ A spectacular hand painted illuminated address, was presented to Mr. & Mrs. J.H. Weatherby senior in 1924, by the employees of J.H. Weatherby & Sons Ltd. It was in celebration of their Diamond Wedding anniversary, and shows photographs of all employees. The original still hangs in an office at the Falcon Pottery.

Our Exhibit at the British Industries Fair, London, 1929.

► J.H. Weatherby & Sons Ltd., exhibited at the British Industry Fairs, and this photograph was taken in London in 1929.

◀ A wonderful photograph taken c1930 on the porch of Mr. J.H. Weatherby's home in Alsager, with three generations of the Weatherby family. From left to right Mr. S.M. Weatherby, Mr. J.S. Weatherby, Mr. J.H. Weatherby senior, Mr. J.L. Weatherby, and Mr. J.H. Weatherby junior.

▶ This photograph was taken in 1991 to celebrate the centenary of J.H. Weatherby & Sons Ltd. From left to right Mr. J.L. Weatherby, Mr J.R. Weatherby, Mr. C.S. Weatherby and seated Mr. J.S. Weatherby. Photograph by The Evening Sentinel.

CHAPTER THREE
THE WEATHERBY WORKERS

When the partnership with Whittaker, Edge & Company was dissolved in 1891, and Mr. J.H. Weatherby senior formed his own company with his sons, some of his former employees joined them in their new business venture. One was Mr. George Cadman, manager of the Falcon Pottery, he was eventually joined by his son A. Cadman and his daughter Ethel Cadman who worked in a secretarial capacity. Mr. Joe Stanway, an artist and designer, also came from Whittaker, Edge to join the Weatherby workforce. When Mr. G. Cadman passed away, Mr. G. Critchley became an efficient manager and stayed with the company for many years.

Mr. W. (Bill) Smith, was a slipmaker with the firm for at least 40 years, he joined in 1898, his father worked for the company before him. Bill Smith presented a gold wristwatch to Mr. John Lucas Weatherby in 1935 on behalf of the workers, at one of the Tea and Social evenings which were so popular before the war. These social evenings were given by the Weatherby family to celebrate any special event, all employees were invited, and the hosts and guests provided their own entertainment.

We have been fortunate to find amongst the Weatherby Archives, photographs taken inside the Falcon Works, dating from before the First World War. These are particularly interesting, not only from the fashion point of view, but also to see the type of wares, and the decorations they were working on.

A later series of photographs were taken about 1931, we are able to name some of the workers in these photographs, thanks to Mr. John Stuart Weatherby and Mrs. Dorothy Gallagher, née Ravenscroft, who worked as a paintress at J.H. Weatherby & Sons Ltd, from 1926 until 1980. We showed the photographs to Dorothy, and were amazed at her ability to recall many names of her fellow workers.

We had an interesting chat with Dorothy, and found she signed her work C. Trent on many of the Woodland Series vases she painted for Weatherby. Her colleague Mrs. May Bentley signed her work T. Edge, these pseudonyms were chosen for them by the decorating manager/designer Mr. Jim Hammond. This was during the 1930s when a piece 'signed by the artist' was considered more saleable.

Dorothy started work in the pottery industry at the age of 13, at the British Art Pottery Co. (Fenton) Ltd, Rialto Works, Fenton, where she was trained, this company closed down in 1926. She worked at Weatherby's for most of her working life apart from 1943 to 1945, when she was conscripted to work at the Rolls Royce factory, making cylinder blocks for the war effort.

Over the years there have been many photographs of retirement presentations to pottery workers, and we have reproduced a few of these. The first such official presentation to take place occurred in 1926, when Mr. J.H. Weatherby junior presented a cheque to Mr. Harry Slater, head mould maker and modeller who had been with the firm for 35 years. The mould maker and modeller has the responsibility of starting the manufacturing process, and it is necessary to be a mathematician to carry out the job properly. This is because it is vital to work out the percentage of shrinkage in the drying and firing process. Harry Slater was an expert, a quiet and charming man.

There was often a reluctance to retire completely, and Harry Millward, the clay manager, was still working part time at the age of 80, he started as an apprentice mould maker under the tutorage of Harry Slater. He joined the company after the First World War, and apart from a short spell in Canada, remained until at least 1991, when he was described in The Evening Sentinel as semi-retired. When the manager, Mr. G. Critchley, passed away, Harry helped the company in every way possible, as he was expert in many departments. Harry Millward passed away in 1993, and was sadly missed by all at the Falcon Pottery.

Mrs. Florrie Wakefield retired at the age of 84, in 1985, and had been in the pottery industry for 71 years, starting at the age of 13, which was normal in those days. In her later years she unlocked the factory every morning at 6 a.m. and it seems she only retired reluctantly because of the cold and snow on wintry mornings. She started as a stilt picker at the Ogdens factory (manufacturers of stilts, spurs and saddles), which adjoined the Falcon Pottery. When they closed in 1948, she crossed the yard from one factory to another and joined Falcon Pottery as a stilt picker until they ceased using the bottle ovens and changed to electric ovens. She then became cleaner, tealady, made sure the management had clean jackets and generally kept everyone in order. She walked to work every morning from Sneyd Green, and was a wonderful character.

Mr. & Mrs. Howell were already working at Weatherby's when they were joined by their daughters Violet and Rose. Rose arrived in 1939 and retired in 1991, she became Mrs. Stanley, and was a sorter and selector. Her sister Violet, became Mrs. Smallwood, she was a cup maker, and able to do many jobs in the cup department. They were, by all accounts, most competent workers. Mr. Howell was assistant to John (Jack) Woodward, fireman, and the family spent all their working life at the Falcon Pottery.

Mr. Horace Wain joined the company as designer and artist in the late 1920's, he was employed for three days a week, one of his designs was the Lustre Ware range, which usually has the special unusual Falcon Ware Crown back stamp. He previously worked for the Cauldon Pottery at Shelton, Hanley, and after the war, opened his own pottery, H.A. Wain & Sons Ltd, Melba Works, Longton, producing a range of earthenware and animals called Melba Ware. Shaw & Copestake (SylvaC) collectors will recognise the name, as they produced matt glazed animals often mistaken for SylvaC Ware.

Frank Clough, a flat plate printer, and Jack Woodward, fireman, completed 50 years service with the company and were officially presented with a retirement cheque in 1945. Frank Clough together with Lottie Slack and her assistant worked as a team for the greater part of Frank's time on the factory. He was a remarkably cheerful man who walked to and from work, Longton to Hanley, starting at 7 a.m. until he retired. He was a most competent operative, happy in his work and most conscientious. His son joined him at the works and worked alongside him as a printer.

John (Jack) Woodward was a biscuit and glost fireman, his assistant or oddman was Mr. J. Howell, (of the family previously mentioned). In those bottle oven days this was an art in itself, the heat had to be carefully controlled, and coal added every three hours. This was a vital part of the production as a quantity of the weeks potting could be ruined by either over-firing or short-firing. Jack was the expert in this particular field, and was one of the highest paid workers at the time, earning £4.8.7d. per week. He fired five glost ovens every fortnight, as well as the biscuit oven which took 80 hours. All sorts of tricks of the trade were used to achieve the correct temperatures, and working constantly in the heat and dust of the ovens must have been exhausting. He retired in 1945 having completed 50 years service with the company.

Tom Broome was the warehouse manager, he lost an arm in the First World War, and consequently spent most days in considerable pain. He became the first man in the potteries to receive the Military Cross, which was presented to him in the Victoria Hall, Hanley at a celebrity concert by Dame Clara Butt, a famous singer of the time. He was an efficient manager, and managed to take 18 dinner plates in his hand, sit on a stool and slide them on to his knee, seeing if there were any faults, turn them over and slide the backs down and discard the faulty ones. He was a remarkable man with incredible strength in his one arm.

Frank Haywood worked in the 1920's as a biscuit placer, and his wife worked in the potting shops. Frank and one other man placed the total output of the potting shops in saggers each week. An oven filled by the weekend was fired during the next week, and became sufficiently cooled to draw out a week on monday. His son Len joined his father and they worked together until Frank and his wife retired. Len continued working with an assistant until he in turn retired. The placing of the saggers was vitally important as any displacement could cause the whole lot to topple over and injure any workers beneath.

Amongst other long service workers were Mrs. Jessie Chadwick 32 years, Mrs. Hilda Bulger 22 years, Tom Healy 50 years, Mabel Brindley 26 years. Other names frequently recalled have been Mr. & Mrs. J. Winkle, A. Simpson and J. Simpson, A. Barker and G. Barker, Mrs. E. Kirkham and A. Kirkham, Mr. J. Price and Mr. F.J. Price, and Anne Bradbury. Many other workers have been identified and named in the illustrated section.

There are an abundance of stories about pottery workers, in fact they really deserve a book to themselves, and we cannot do them justice or mention everyone who deserves to be mentioned in this one chapter. Suffice it to say for the time being, they were hard working and dedicated members of the Weatherby team.

▲ This photograph was taken in the packing house c.1931. Tom Broome the warehouse manager is on the left, he lost an arm in the First World War and was the first man in the Potteries to receive the Military Medal, presented by Dame Clara Butt. He suffered constant pain because of his injuries and was a brave and gallant man. He was a good singer and was one of the entertainers at the Tea and Social gatherings. Second from left is the packers assistant who is putting straw between each plate, this went into the crate which was made of willow. In the centre is packer Len Curzon preparing to straw a crate in which goods were sent abroad. Len Curzon helped Bill Smith with the coming-of-age presentation to the young Mr. Weatherbys', and was with the company a number of years. Harold Kelsall is on the right.

▲ The decorating department at J.H. Weatherby & Sons Ltd., c1914, note the mode of dress and hairstyles.

▼ The glazing department c1914.

◀ Bowl, cup, saucer and plate making department c1914.

▼ Making cups and bowls c1931, possibly in the same location as the 1914 photograph.

▲ Clay presses in the slip house. Bill Smith on the left worked for the company for at least 40 years, joining in 1898. His father also worked for the company before him. He presented a gold wristwatch to John Stuart Weatherby and John Lucas Weatherby on the occasion of their coming of age. On the right of the picture is Bob Brant. c1931.

▼ Dipping and glazing department, Sam Johnson, hollow ware dipper, on the left is about to pass a piece of ware to his assistant for placing on a ribbed board. c1931. Sam Johnson entertained with a song at the Tea and Social gatherings.

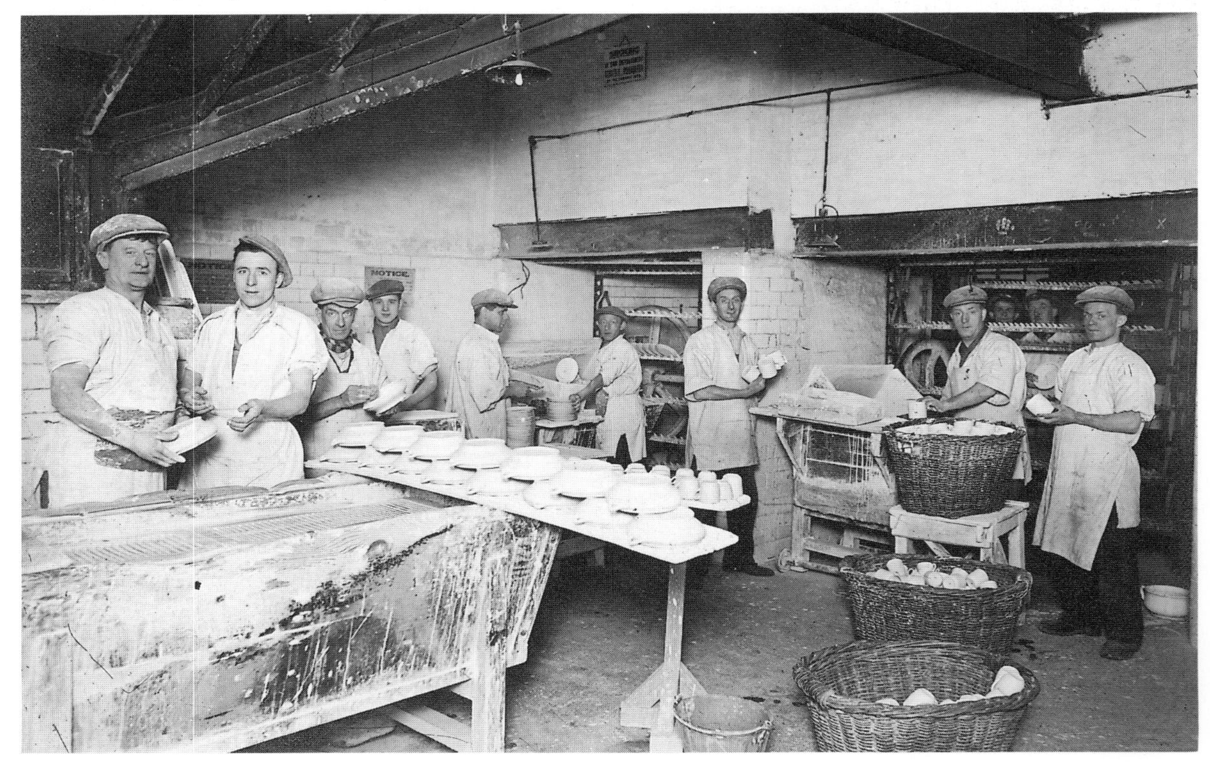

▲ Plate making department, Jack Shannier in the foreground c1931. Probably the same location as the c1914 photograph.

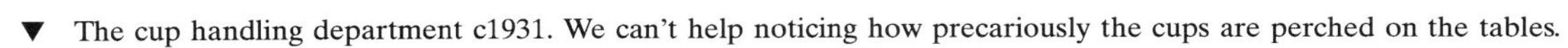

▼ The cup handling department c1931. We can't help noticing how precariously the cups are perched on the tables.

▲ From left, Sid Barnet, Len Barnet and Jack Woodward oven fireman in the saggar making department c1931. You can see Jack dressed up for his retirement presentation on one of the following pages.

◀ Placing saggars in the oven c1931. Tom Badderley second from right is the leader of the team of glost placers.

▲ Printing and transferring the patterns c1931. Frank Clough, the printer is on the left. Second from right in the foreground is Charlotte (Lottie) Slack. Frank can be seen receiving his retirement cheque on one of the following pages.

▼ In the aerographing department. From second right are Dora Gotham, Cathy Green, Elsie Wolley, Hilda Love. On the right is Mr. John Lucas Weatherby c1931.

▲ Here we see Hilda Weston, Lily Mare, Annie Stevenson, Madge Heath, Betty Caulder, Marie McNulty (a singer at the Tea and Social gathering), Ivy Mare, Elsie Hill, Doris Barker, Vera Hopkinson, Rose Galligher, Lily Stanway and others busy in the decorating department c1931. Compare this with the c1914 photograph.

▼ On the left is Mabel Rowley, Gladys Stimson is fourth from right, Harold Kelsall third from right, in the glost warehouse are sorters and selectors. Tom Broome on the right is the warehouse manager. c1931.

▲ Mr. J.H. Weatherby junior presenting cheques to Mr. John (Jack) Woodward, oven fireman, and Mr. Frank Clough, printer, on the completion of 50 years service. c1946.

◀ Mrs. Jessie Chadwick, left, with 32 years service and Mrs. Hilda Bulger, right with 22 years service, being presented with cheques by Mr. J. Stuart Weatherby and Mr. J. Lucas Weatherby in 1982. Looking on are Mr. Jonathan Weatherby, Mr. Christopher Weatherby and Mr. Albert Hall, works manager. (Newspaper cutting by courtesy of The Evening Sentinel).

◄ Mrs. Florrie Wakefield was 84 years old when this photograph was taken in the Weatherby showroom in 1985. She had worked at the Falcon Pottery for 38 years, and in the pottery industry for 71 years. (Newspaper cutting by courtesy of The Evening Sentinel).

► Mrs. Dorothy Gallagher in 1995, holding two examples of her work whilst at the Falcon Pottery. She signed her work C. Trent, and was employed as a paintress from 1926–1980.

◄ Mrs. Rose Stanley, left, with 54 years service, Mr. Tom Healey, 50 years service and Mrs. Mabel Brindley, 26 years service, being presented with cheques by Mr. J. Lucas Weatherby and Mr. J. Stuart Weatherby in 1991. Looking on are Mr. Jonathan Weatherby and Christopher Weatherby. (Newspaper cutting by courtesy of The Evening Sentinel).

CHAPTER FOUR
PRODUCTS OF THE FACTORY

Products at the Pinnox Works, Pinnox Street, Tunstall, in 1891, consisted of toilet sets, vases, tableware, described as '***General Earthenware, plain, printed and decorated suitable for the Home and Foreign Markets.***' '***The valuable services of the artist Mr. J. Stanway,***' were also secured, '***so the newest designs and best shapes could be introduced***'. Mr. Stanway had been employed at Whittaker, Edge & Co, where Mr. J.H. Weatherby senior had previously been a partner. The back stamp of the Union Jack flag with 'durability' through the centre was devised, with the words 'J.H.W. & Sons, Tunstall, England'. The decoration names were also shown above the flag, such as 'Floral' and 'Peony', the Registered Design Number was sometimes included. The colour of the backstamp varied in accordance with the colour of the decoration.

Similar wares continued to be produced a year later when the factory moved to the Falcon Pottery, High Street, Hanley in September 1892. The range of shapes were gradually increased, they had a very popular line of chamber pots with matching lids! The original decoration pattern books are still kept at the works, and we were astounded at the variety available, all beautifully hand painted, and of very high quality. The flag trade mark continued to be used, but the place name 'Hanley' replaced 'Tunstall'.

The earliest pattern book found on the Falcon Pottery premises is dated 2nd September 1899. The pattern numbers ranged between 499 and 8,000+ and were gradually discontinued. In the 1899 pattern book illustrations included vases, jugs, cheese dishes, teapots, butterdishes, plates, fernpots on feet and triple plates. The pattern or decoration number would be neatly hand-painted on the base of the ware, for identification purposes. Each example pattern was actually hand painted into the pattern book in colour, one painting per page, making a magnificent record of artwork for the company.

The fact that the pattern books survived a terrible fire in 1910 is surprising. This disaster happened in the early hours of November 4th, when the south portion of the works was found to be on fire. The main portion of the pottery was saved, but the sagger house, two glost ovens, one printing shop, two gilding shops, one pressing shop, a dipping house, drying room, mould-makers shop and block and case stores were all destroyed. 200 workers were temporarily unemployed. All the departments affected were well stocked at the time and the destruction of the blocks and cases and the copper plates used for printing was a serious loss. Fortunately this loss was covered by insurance, and the factory eventually recovered from this setback, and the works returned to normal.

They produced much table ware, one of the most popular dinner services available was Empress shape with 'Belmont' pattern, in colours Flo Canton, Pea Blue and Sage Green, with or without Gold Edge. This service came in three sizes of 26, 54, or 61 pieces. On one of the early adverts it is described thus: '***This is a LIVE PATTERN it keeps MOVING.***' Mr. F. Clough, printer, and Mrs. Charlotte (Lottie) Slack printed Belmont pattern in flo-blue non-stop for 14 years before 1920. (So says a little note attached to one of the items.) Sometimes dinner services were even required in sets of 112 pieces. The pattern numbers for this pre-First World War era reached in the region of 3000 some patterns were named only, as 'Hudson' and 'Chatsworth', a few were named and numbered.

From the 1920's and 1930's Weatherby's produced many fashionable Art Deco style vases, as well as tableware, and superb wall plaques, but although they produced a variety of 'fancy' lines these were simply regarded as supplementary to their 'Utility' wares which they continued to produce at competitive prices. A large percentage of wares were exported to Canada, Australia and America, these were bought by the crate and demand was so great it was necessary for customers orders to be rationed.

In 1920 a lucrative market was found for supplying wares to the hotel and catering trades. This gradually extended to any establishment requiring large amounts of crockery such as ocean liners, hospitals, institutions etc.

In 1934 'The Woodpecker Ware' tableware range was introduced, this is highly sought after today, as is 'Harvest Time' tableware with embossed sheafs of corn with poppies and cornflowers. They also experimented with matt glazes which were proving so popular with the general public. The style of wares had changed considerably by this time, as customers required dainty prints and shapes for their teasets. Some nursery ware was produced, which consisted of nursery rhyme designs with a green edge. The production of ornate Victorian and Edwardian designs with heavy gilding had come to an end.

Handpainting still continued on many of the wares and there are stunning examples of these on the handpainted advertising cards the sales representatives took with them on their travels. In 1938 200 workers were still employed at the Falcon Pottery, but these numbers were to decrease dramatically at the start of the war. During the war years only white ware could be supplied to the home market, decorated ware was for export only. The majority of workers were called up or required to work in munitions factories or other industries associated with the war effort. Most of the decorators were dispersed to other work, or retired, never to have the opportunity of returning to their trade.

The following is an extract from the Pottery Gazette dated November 1941 under the heading '***Concentration of the Pottery Industry in North Staffordshire: J.H. Weatherby & Sons Ltd, Falcon Pottery, Hanley, Stoke-on-Trent. Concentration here is with the Wulstan Pottery Ltd, Sefton Pottery, Hanley, who will be closing down their works and centring production along with Weatherbys at the Falcon Pottery. Although it may be necessary, under concentration, to cut out certain shapes in order to achieve all possible output and to cope with the increased demand for export, both firms will be carrying on much as usual, though on restricted output. Weatherbys will continue to manufacture their non-crazing earthenware in general dinner and teaware and fancies, and will continue the manufacture of hotelware and suitable lines for the catering trade, canteens and hospitals.***'

Because of the Government restrictions and shortage of man-power, the machinery manufacturers produced semiautomatic machines to complete the operations. This meant two operatives could produce the same number of plates as three previously, heralding the first major changes in the pottery industry.

Before the war a decorating manager was employed to oversee the decorating department, checking the quality of the work. During the war years this was discontinued, and after this period freelance designers visited the factory producing their own ideas and styles, some of which were purchased and used by the factory. In 1949 the decorating shops were completely gutted by fire, these were eventually rebuilt, together with a new canteen.

The large dinner, tea and fruit sets, were now discontinued, as customers required combined sets. The hotel ware side of the business, although good before the war, increased greatly after the war, and they also concentrated on fancy goods and souvenir ware, all of which benefited from being shown at the trade fair in Blackpool.

The Diamond Jubilee of the firm was celebrated in 1951, this was marked by the introduction of a new shape of dinner and tea ware called Princess. Also during the 1950's and 1960's, animals and figures were modelled for the first time. (See Chapter seven). The gift ware and souvenir trade started to take off in a big way during this decade, and still continues to be a large part of the Falcon Ware production. The Falcon Ware colourful Union Jack trade mark can be found on souvenirs from all over the world.

The 1960's was a busy innovative decade as new ranges of table ware were introduced, including June Ware, a particularly attractive range with embossed flowers, in a honey or mother of pearl glaze. This was originally bought from another pottery, G.M. Creyke & Sons, Bell Works, Hanley, when the works closed down in 1948. (This is now the site of the City Museum and Art Gallery, Hanley). It is possible this range was produced at Weatherby's earlier than the decoration number 7918 (c1962) indicates, Mr. J.S. Weatherby believes this is so, and possibly it was originally produced without a decoration number, and given one at a later date.

Another exclusive 1960's design was the range of Brownie Downing nursery ware, pink and white for girls and blue and white for boys. Decorated with six child studies called European Childrens Series, these had a special Brownie Downing back stamp, and were by an Australian designer. Brownie Downing designs are also found on the ever popular Tilly trays, which are small dishes used for sweets or ashtrays, and can be found in vast quantities for just a few pounds or pence each, but great fun for collectors. The rarer decorations such as Butlins, Dalek, or Thelwell designs, are more desirable and consequently demand a higher price.

From about 1963 the flag trade mark incorporated the date of production on some gift ware and hotel ware. This is particularly useful when being told by a dealer that the item in question is 1930's!

During the 1970's production of hotel and gift ware continued to increase, but the animals, figures and vases so popular two decades before, ceased to be manufactured. A popular 1970's tableware range was the White Wheat range, this is a traditional tableware design used by many world wide manufacturers. There is even a book devoted to the subject called The Wheat Pattern, an Illustrated Survey, by Lynne Sussman, published by the Canadian Government Publishing Centre, Quebec, Canada, in which the Falcon Ware White Wheat range is mentioned. Weatherbys supplied the White Wheat range to the Laura Ashley company for some time.

During the 1980's the Hallfield Collection, (in the 1890's Mr. J.H. Weatherby senior had a partnership in the Hallfield Pottery), was introduced, which featured reproductions of 19th Century multi-coloured printed designs. Each scene was decorated from a set of new hand engraved copper plates to bring out the detail and subtle colours.

In 1991 to celebrate their centenary, the Celebration range of wall plates was introduced, the plates were overlaid with an elaborate or plain border of 22ct gold, with a wide choice of centre designs.

Weatherby's will make any designs to customers own specifications. Now, as in the early days, they are still well known for their hotel ware, and in 1995 they celebrated seventy-five years in this particular field. The gift and souvenir trade forms a strong part of their business at home and overseas, and almost everyone must have come across a Falcon Ware wall plate, mug or tray when souvenir hunting or looking for a suitable gift. When necessary commemorative pieces are also available, and have been throughout the decades. Exports continue to increase, particularly to America, and are now over 20% of the output. As J.H. Weatherby & Sons Ltd have been in business for 105 years this year (1996), it is not surprising they have strong business links and a good reputation all over the world.

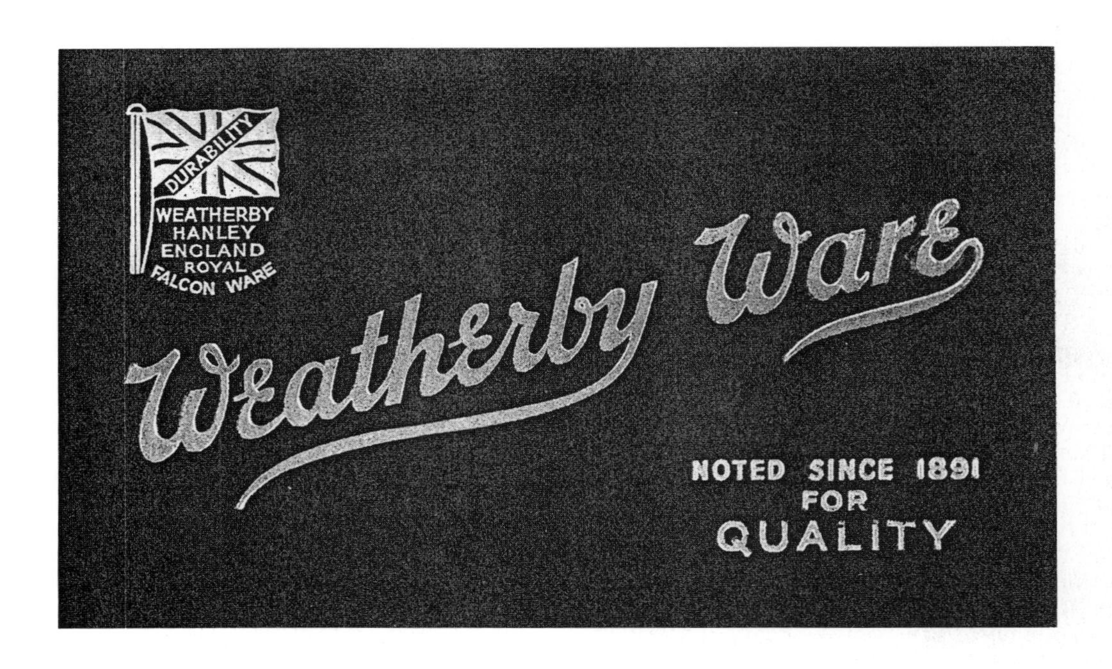

Toilet ware produced by J. H. Weatherby & Sons, at the Pinnox Works, Tunstall, between 1891 and 1892. The 'Peony' decoration.

▲ A jar made at the Pinnox Works, 1891–1892, the 'Peony' decoration has a red flower and brown leaves.

▲ Made at the Pinnox Works, 1891–1892, with a blue 'Peony' decoration.

▼ Teapot with 'Floral' decoration made at the Pinnox Works, it has the Registered number 163002. All items on this page from the Weatherby Collection.

These are the style of decorations available c1903.

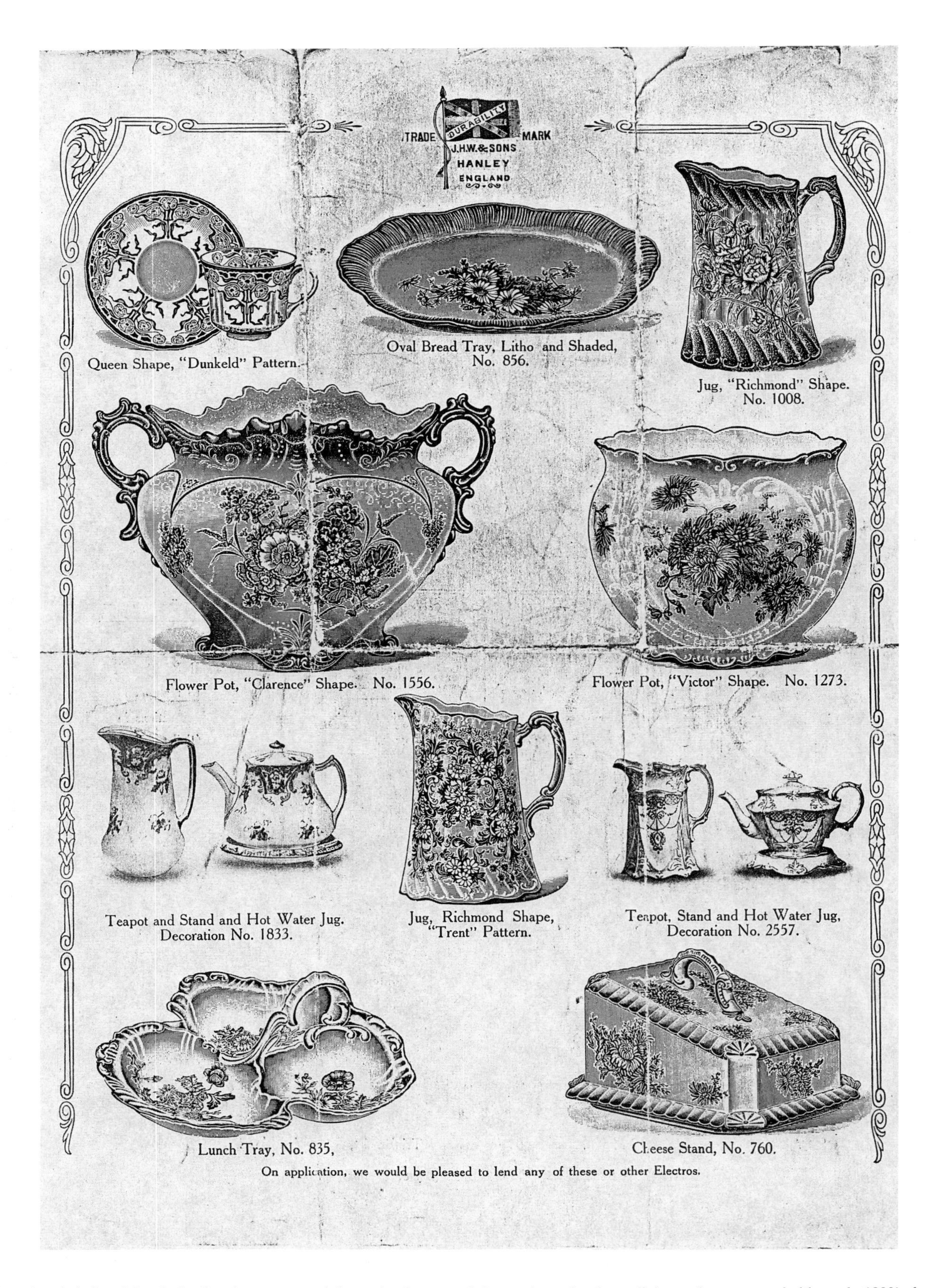

TRADE MARK
DURABILITY
J.H.W. & SONS
HANLEY
ENGLAND
Queen Shape, "Dunkeld" Pattern.
Oval Bread Tray, Litho and Shaded, No. 856.
Jug, "Richmond" Shape. No. 1008.
Flower Pot, "Clarence" Shape. No. 1556.
Flower Pot, "Victor" Shape. No. 1273.
Teapot and Stand and Hot Water Jug. Decoration No. 1833.
Jug, Richmond Shape, "Trent" Pattern.
Teapot, Stand and Hot Water Jug, Decoration No. 2557.
Lunch Tray, No. 835,
Cheese Stand, No. 760.
On application, we would be pleased to lend any of these or other Electros.

This rather faded and fragile leaflet shows some of the early shapes and decorations, the three digit numbers are probably early 1900's, but the teapot, decoration number 2557, indicates it was still in use at a later date.

It has not been possible to date this leaflet exactly, but judging by the decoration numbers we think it is probably pre-1918.

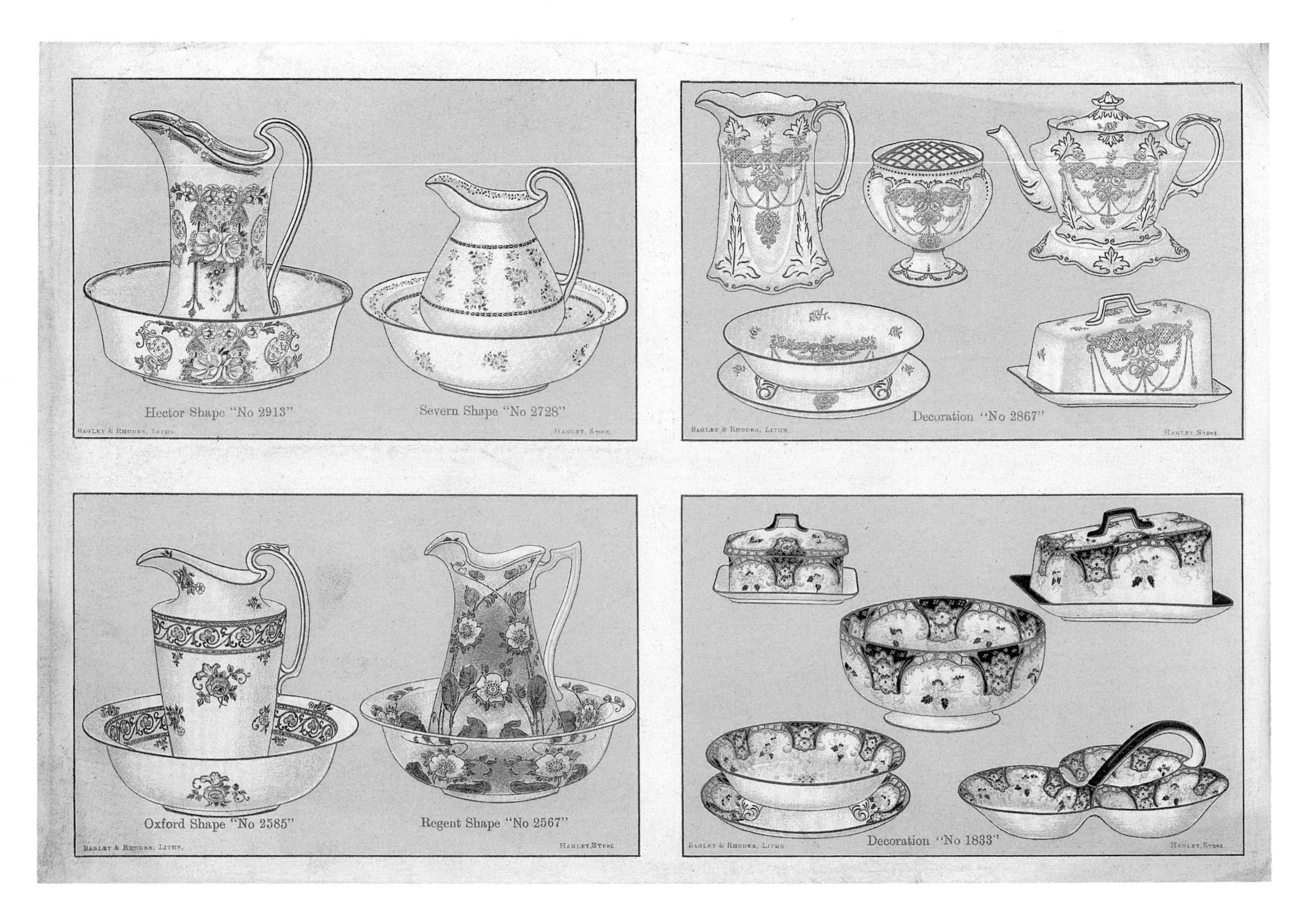

The decoration numbers give us a rough guide as to the date of this leaflet, which we think is probably pre-1918.

No. 3569. Underglaze Mazarine Blue Band and Gold, with Hair Brown Doric Festoon Print.

These designs are c1920, when hotel ware started to become the mainstay of Weatherby production.

ROSEDALE No. 4401.

A good selection of 1930's shapes in the Rosedale pattern.

Some striking 1930's designs and jug shapes.

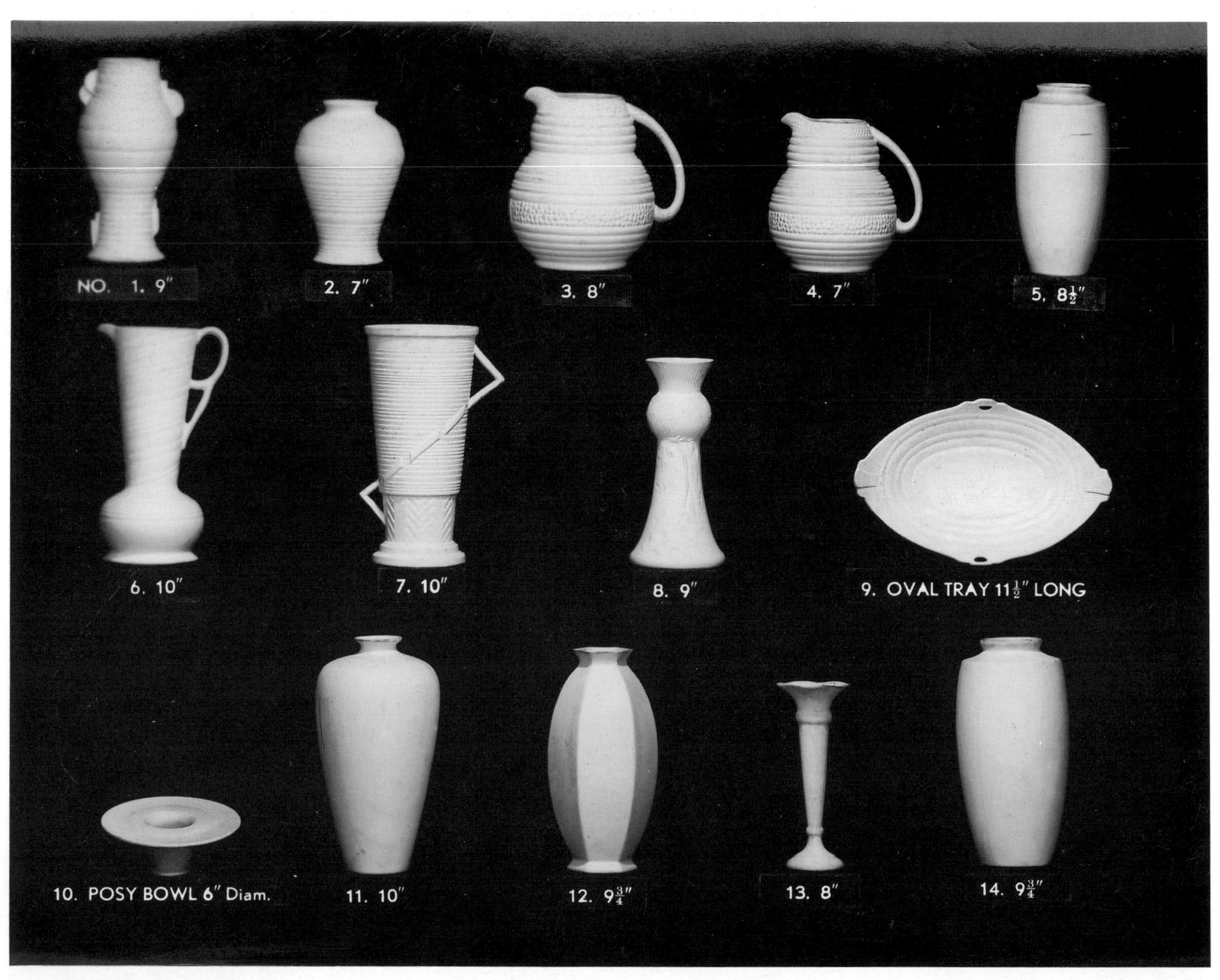

During the 1930's shape numbers were given to vases, but some of these shapes had been used earlier and given names.

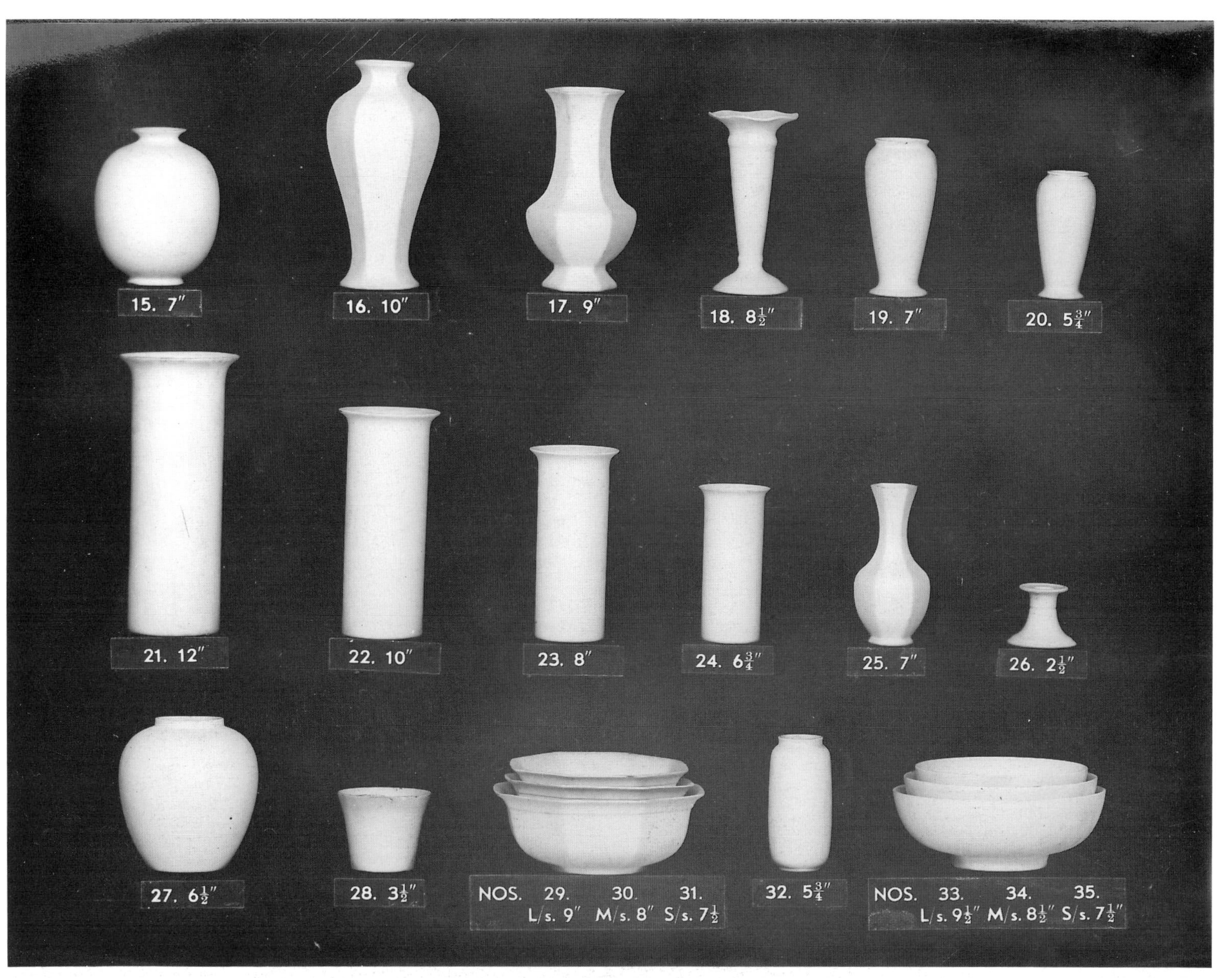

Although these wares were only given numbers during the 1930's, some had been used previously and given shape names.

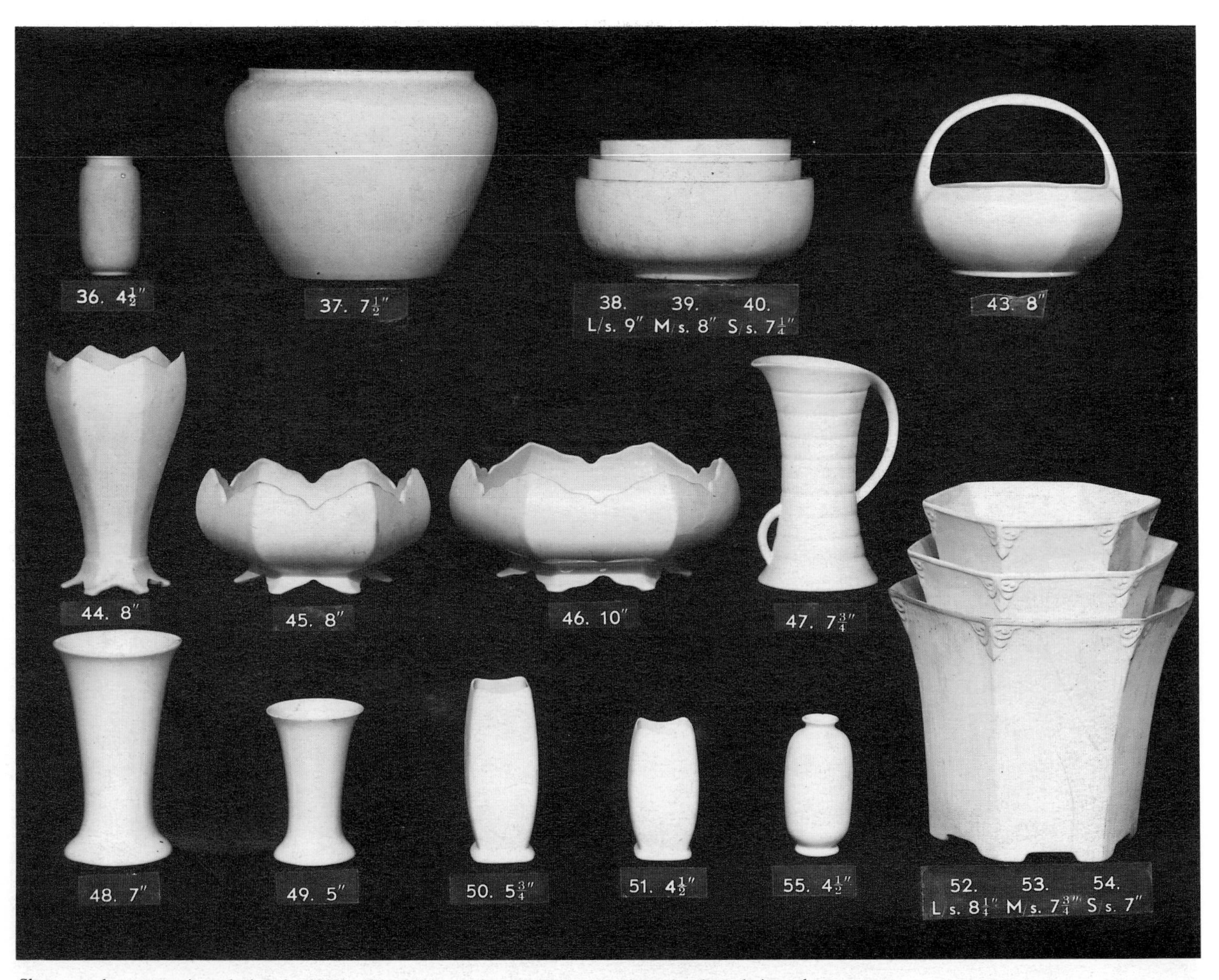

Shape numbers were given during the 1930's, although some shapes had been used previously and given shape names.

An interesting selection of 1930's shapes with a definite Art Deco influence, number 62 has the typical 'Odeon' look.

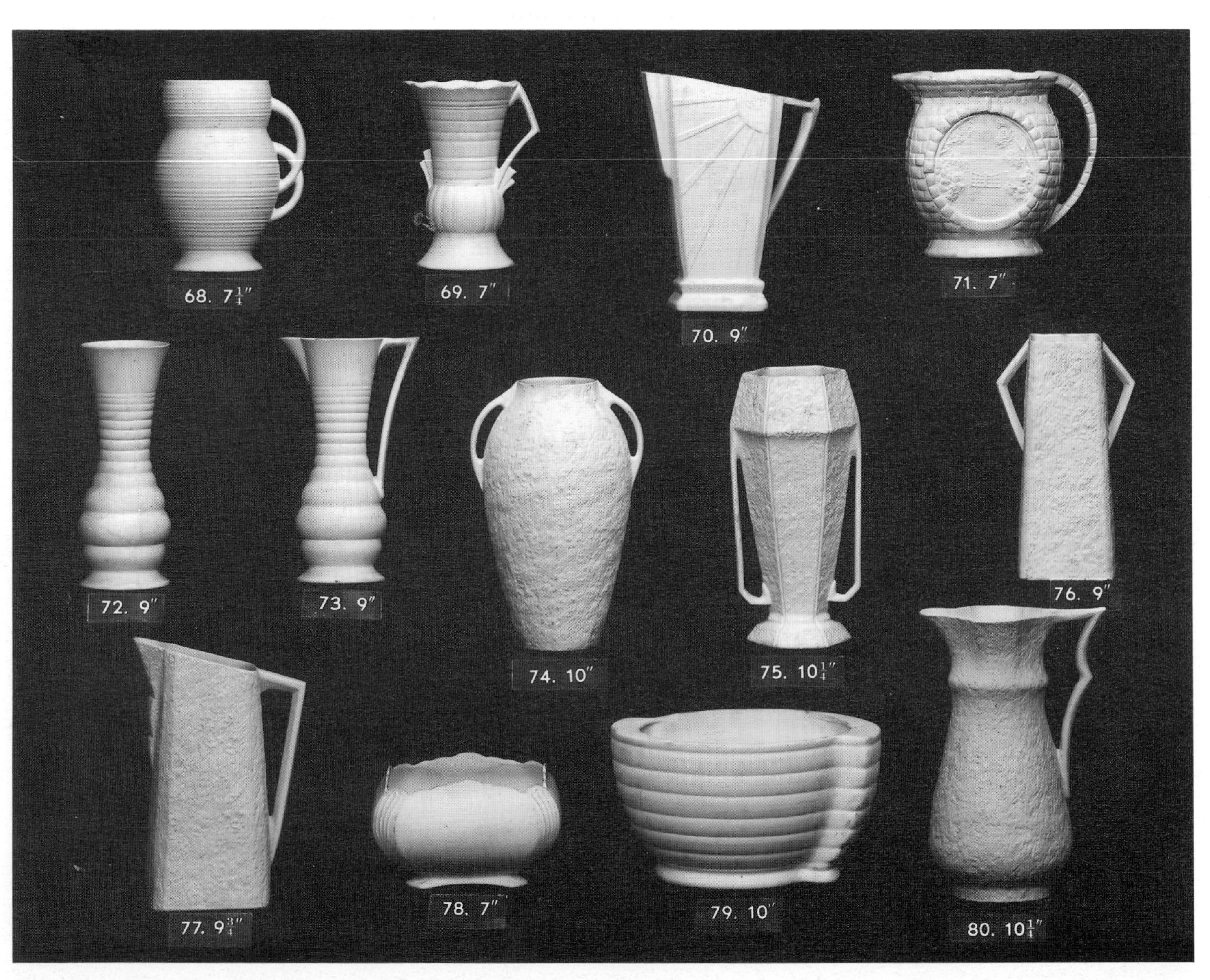

Some 1930's designs in Art Deco style, particularly number 70 with the sunray effect.

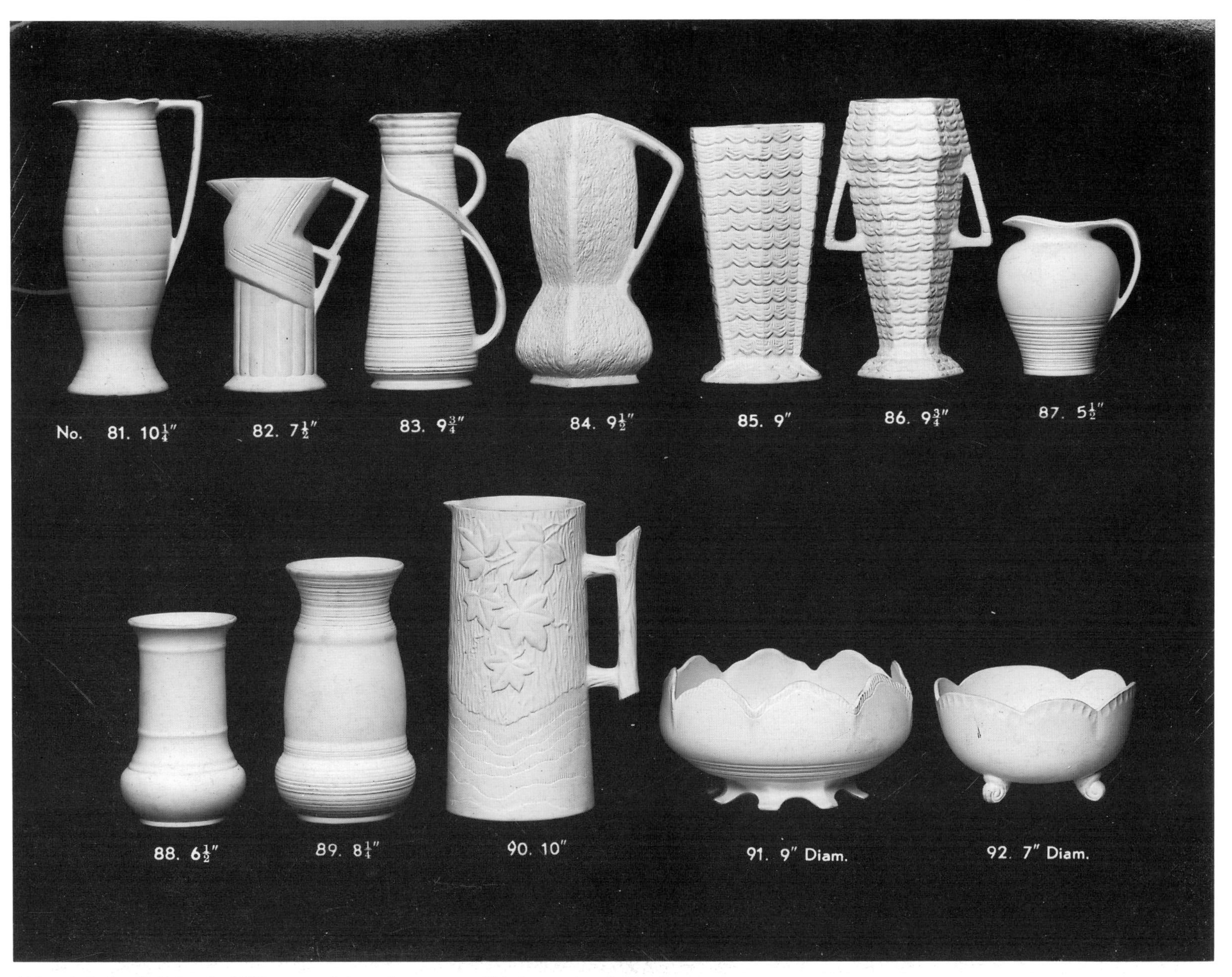

Although designed during the 1930's some of these shapes were still being produced after the war.

▲ Handpainted vase signed T. Edge (aka May Bentley) decoration number 5760, The Woodland Series c1937.

▲ We found this damaged vase number 67, amongst the Weatherby Collection and thought the handpainted decoration stunning.

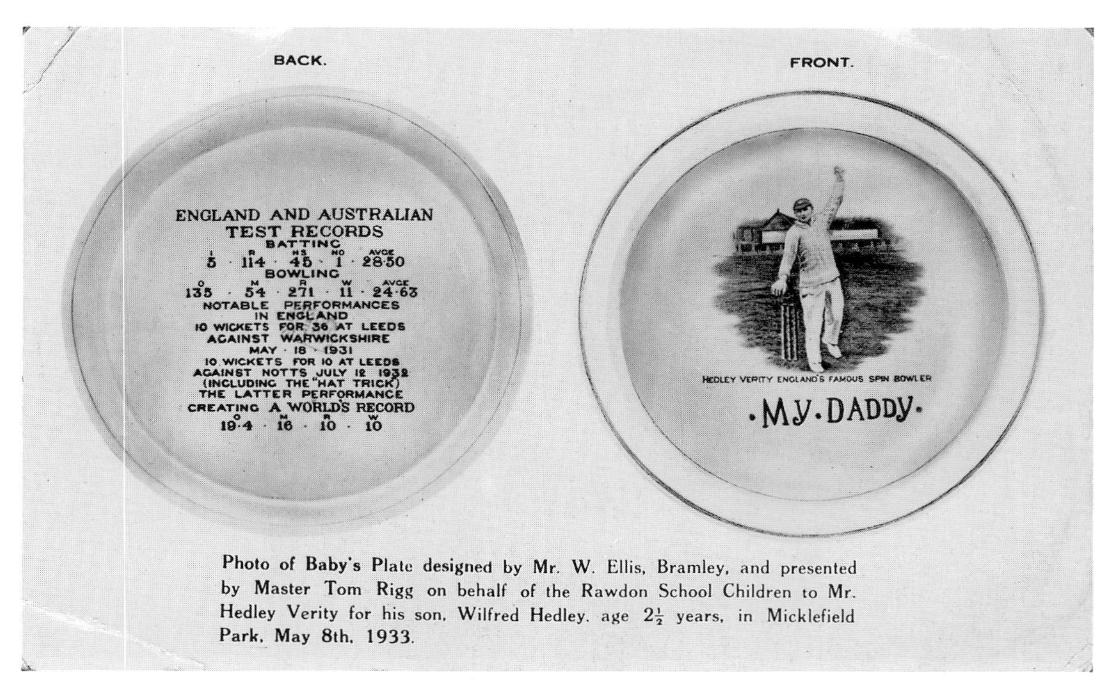

▲ A 'special' made by Weatherbys in 1933.

◀ Triangular plate number 65 in an attractive green, black and cream pattern, beautifully set off on a chrome stand complete with butter knife c1935.

▼ Cake plate number 440, with the delightful Water Lily decoration number 6561 c1950.

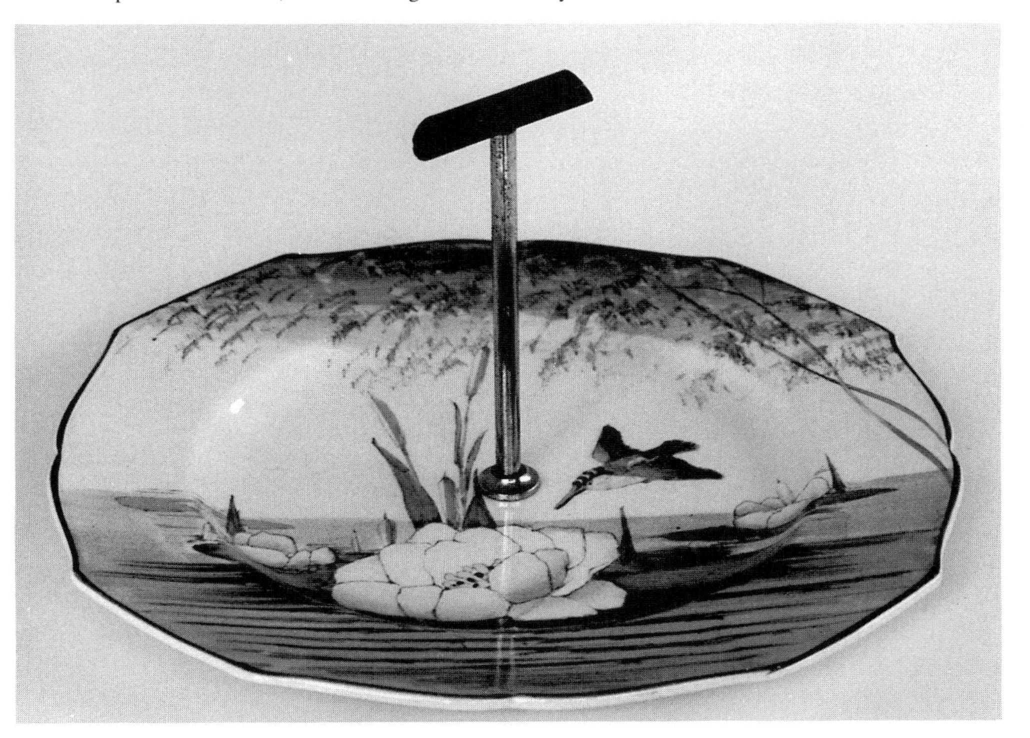

◄ Cake plate number 139, with embossed fruit similar to the pot below. We have found other items in this design, including a cake stand, and oval dish. The pattern number is 6329 c1945.

► This pot is embossed with fruit and flowers, and has a crazy paving effect. An orange acts as the lid knob. The decoration number is 5739, it is 3¾″ high to knob and 5″ diameter. c1937.

◄ Teapot from the Delphine range, the name is incised on the base, it is 6″ high. There are other items in this range, including a cheese dish, bowl, sandwich plate and honey pot. We can't be sure about the date of this range as it has no decoration number, but it is very similar to June Ware c1962. From the Weatherby Collection.

◄ Sandwich plate and cup and saucer with the 'Pink Lady' decoration number 7033 c1955. Usually found on Princess shape tableware, a universally popular theme.

► A chrome fruit bowl stand containing bowl and desert dishes with a different yellow crinoline lady decoration number 6895 or 6875 c1952. A popular decoration found on various tableware, including cake stands and cake plates.

◄ Part of a yellow crinoline lady tea set decoration number 6895 or 6875 c1952.

▲ The sugar sifter 4¾″ high and the honey pot 3½″ high are an interesting shape. Another collector also has a bowl with a chrome lid in this shape which is 2½″ high and 5¾″ diameter. The style of decorations are c1950.

▼ Vase number 121 painted by Mrs. Dorothy Gallagher who kindly presented it to me when we visited her. c1960.

▼ Moongate wall plaque, similar to vase number 71 possibly made around the same time c1935. From the Weatherby Collection.

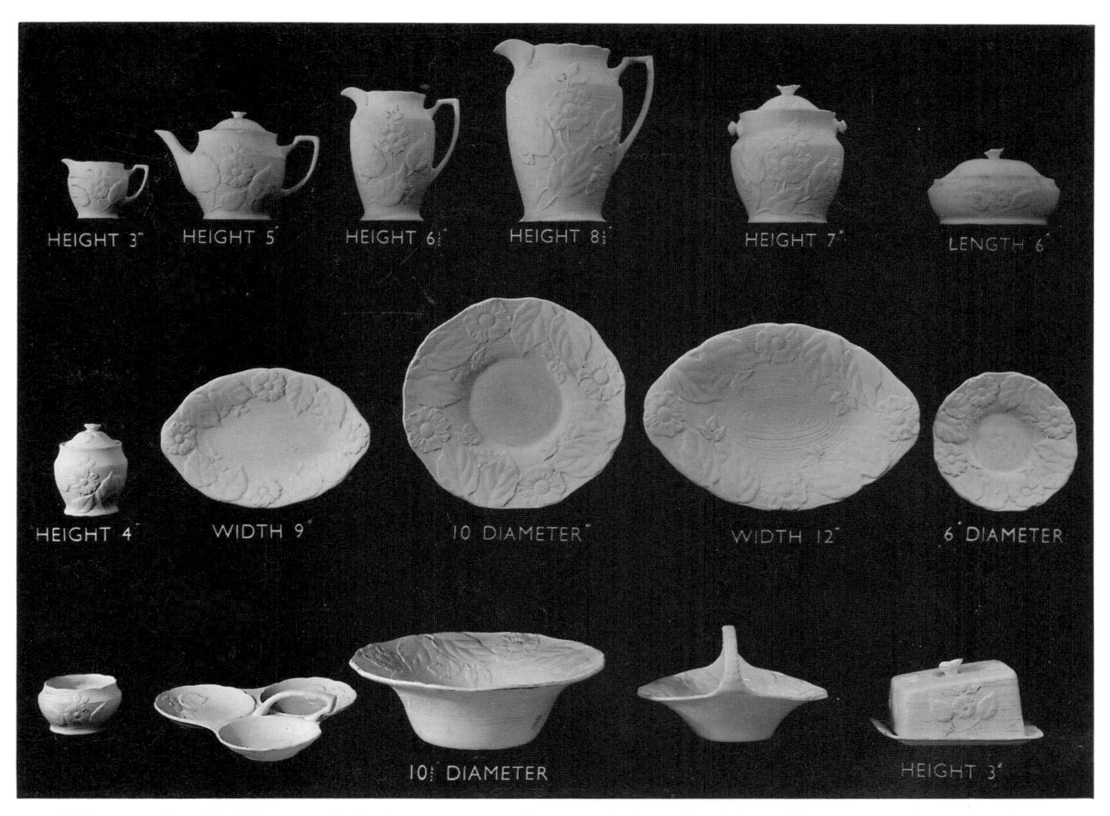

▲ This range is called Rosa, and the honey pot can be seen in the colour section. The decoration numbers are 6429, 7096 and 7097, depending on the colours used. c1949–1956.

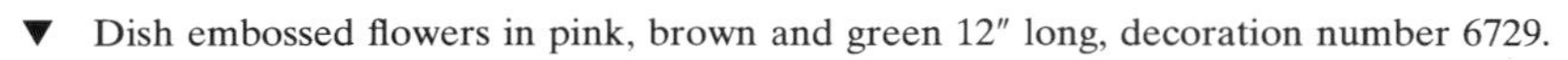
▼ Dish embossed flowers in pink, brown and green 12″ long, decoration number 6729.

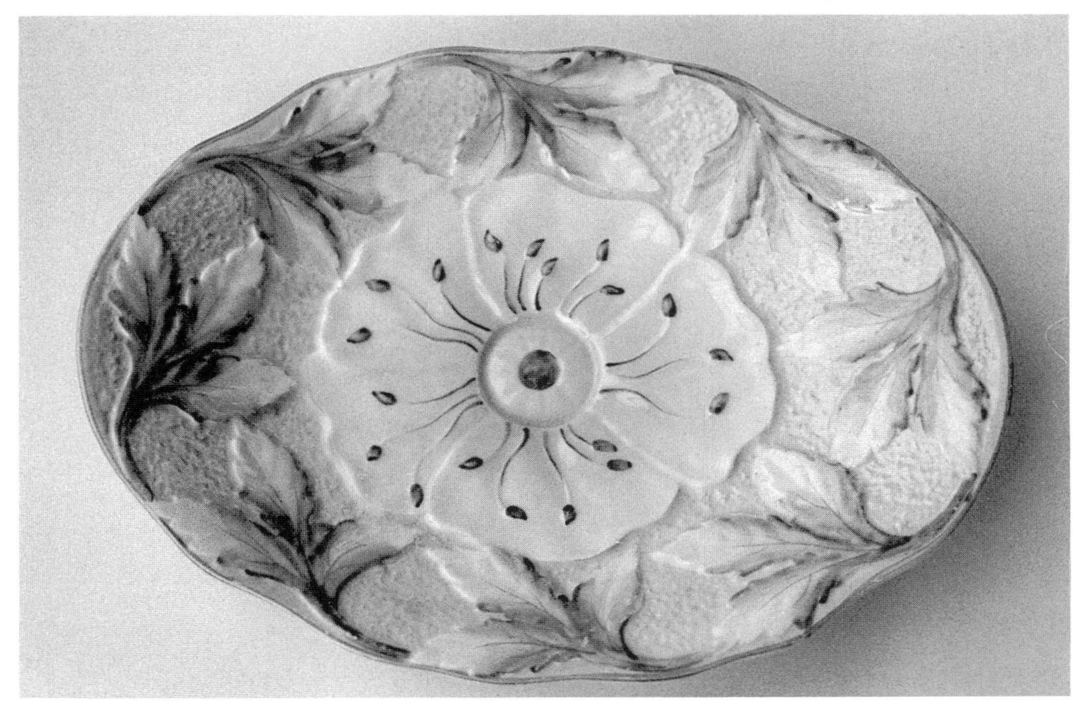

These shapes were produced during the 1950's and 1960's and continued until the 1970's, you will see them sometimes in satin or matt glazes.

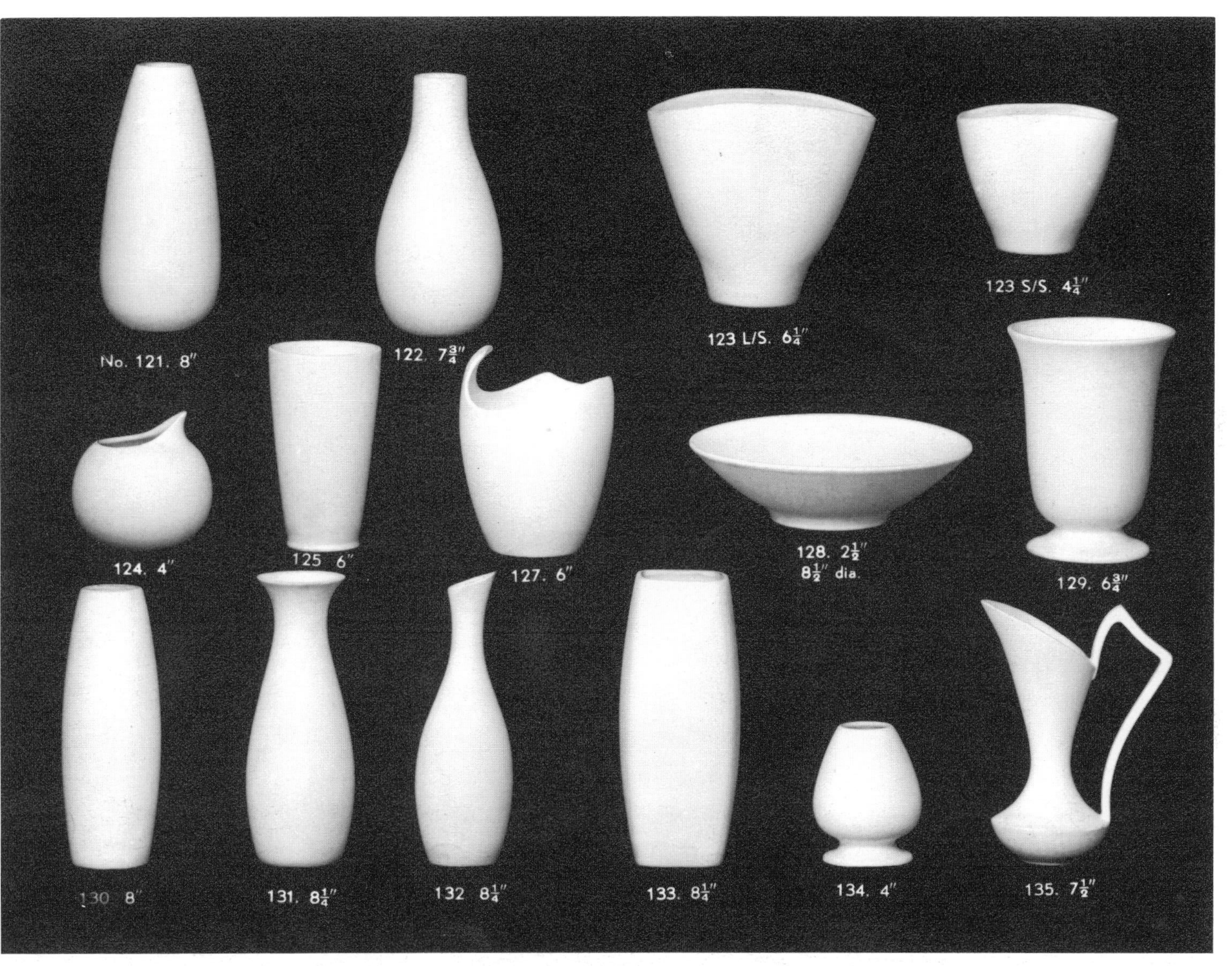

Typical 1950's and 1960's shapes, some of which were used for the Brownie Downing Series.

NURSERY WARE

. . . exclusively by WEATHERBY

Nursery Ware by Brownie Downing introduces an attractive new selection to this exclusive Weatherby range. Available in sets of Pink and White for little girls and Blue and White for little boys, Brownie Downing nursery ware will be a sure favourite with all your customers. Write now for full details, prices and fascinating life story of BROWNIE DOWNING.

J. H. WEATHERBY & SONS LTD.,
Falcon Pottery, Hanley, Staffs.

Tel: Stoke-on-Trent 23711/2

599

First produced in the 1960's, the Nursery Ware is rarer than the other Brownie Downing items.

▲ Cactus Ware biscuit barrel 6″ high 5″ diameter, from the collection of and photograph by Jackie and Tony Chew.

▲ Cactus Ware jug 6½″–7″ high belongs to Mrs. Dorothy Gallagher.

▼ Cactus Ware dish 11½″ long. The decoration number is not easy to read, and could be 6916 or 7167. c1957. Also in this range is a cheese dish, butter dish, teapot, and honey pot.

▲ Mug commemorating the silver jubilee of Queen Elizabeth II 1977, jug decorated with flowers 5¼″ high dated 1974, tankard dated 1969 inscribed on the back 'The Bulls Head Hotel, Congleton, Olde Englishe Nyte, Pro. A. Cropper'.

▼ A selection of Tilly dishes, including commemorative, humourous and advertising, there are many different designs, and we have over 50 in our collection. They first appeared on the scene in 1962, and are still being made.

▲ Weatherbys have produced many interesting plates. We particularly liked this one, called 'Riverina', which has an interesting back stamp, c1949 (see chapter on back stamps). From the Weatherby Collection.

▲ This plate is one of many found by Paul and Denise Tripp, who kindly look out for interesting pieces for us. It is very colourful, and fortunately dated.

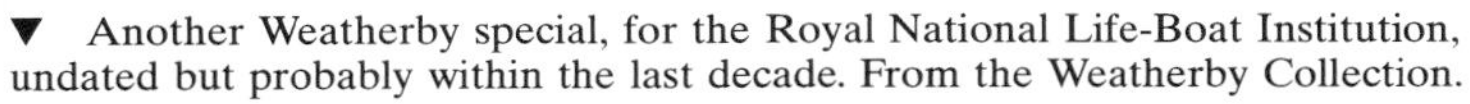

▼ Another Weatherby special, for the Royal National Life-Boat Institution, undated but probably within the last decade. From the Weatherby Collection.

CONSORT 8220 | CONSORT 8221 | CONSORT 8219 | TOBAGO | SPRING MIST | CONSORT 8221

Above is a selection from our new range of Victoriana. Initially the collection comprises Atlas Jug, Vase, Octagon Jug (all illustrated top row), Rose Bowl, Plant Pot and Candy Box (bottom row). Five decorations are available: Consort 8219; Consort 8220; Consort 8221; Spring Mist and Tobago. All the shapes are available in all the decorations.

Below is a selection of our popular banded and gilt range of wall plates. There are four different coloured bands and they are available with more than sixty different series of centres. The centres include Hunting scenes, Game Birds, Florals, Country Inns etc and the plates are supplied loose or gift boxed.

TOP ROW: PLATE 10" | SERVICE PLATE | PLATE 9" | DOUBLE BOXED BUTTER PADS

BOTTOM ROW: BUTTER PADS BOXED | ROUND TRINKET BOX | OVAL DISH 12" | ROUND TRINKET BOX | PLATE 6½"

J. H. WEATHERBY & SONS LTD

Falcon Pottery · Town Road · Hanley · Stoke-on-Trent · Staffordshire · Telephone: 0782 23711/2

A Weatherby advertising leaflet showing a range of reproduction Victoriana, plates and trinket boxes, c1963.

WE SPECIALISE IN SPECIALS!

We were among the first pottery manufacturers to produce "specials" and we still lead the field with our very wide range of ware which can be decorated with any design to suit the customer. We can work from a picture postcard, letterheading or other illustration or we can prepare a special design for you. You will be pleasantly surprised at our economic prices, even for modest quantities.

The Weatherby Specials Service complements our Weatherby Giftware range

J. H. WEATHERBY & SONS LTD

Falcon Pottery · Town Road · Hanley · Stoke-on-Trent · Staffordshire · Telephone: 0782 23711/2

A Weatherby advertising leaflet showing a selection of their Specials, circa early 1960's.

The Perfect Present

From the heart of Staffordshire, centre of the world's pottery industry, Weatherby Giftware, established in 1891, brings you a unique blend of traditional craftsmanship, stylish designs and first class service. The Weatherby collection is extremely comprehensive and carries the ideal range for you and your customer.

WEATHERBY GIFTWARE

Falcon Pottery, Town Road, Hanley, Stoke-On-Trent ST1 2LB Tel: (0782) 23711/2

Manufacturers since 1891

A Weatherby advertising leaflet showing a good selection of their gift ware range, circa early 1980's.

CHAPTER FIVE
COMMEMORATIVE AND BADGED WARE

ROYAL COMMEMORATIVES

The earliest Royal commemorative mug we have found is the Silver Jubilee of King George V and Queen Mary in 1935, but no doubt there are other earlier examples. Jackie and Tony Chew, who enjoy collecting Weatherby Ware, have found three examples of cups produced to celebrate the coronation of Queen Elizabeth II, in 1953.

In 1969, a beautiful range of large decorated plates was produced for the Investiture of H.R.H. Prince Charles as Prince of Wales at Caernarvon Castle. We have seen three very impressive examples with borders in blue and gold, red and gold and green and gold.

There are several designs of Queen Elizabeth II Silver Jubilee 1977 commemoratives, appropriately the Princess shape was used for the beaker, but other shapes as well as plates and small dishes were also used. Although some items have a decoration which was for general use, Weatherby's also commissioned a special design for their use only, which is quite distinctive. A blue and white plate was produced featuring London landmarks, surrounding the Queen's head in the centre. It has a blue back stamp with the words Silver Jubilee Pride over a crown, under the crown are the words CAPITAL PLATE, MADE BY WEATHERBY HANLEY ENGLAND.

For the wedding of H.R.H. Prince Charles and Lady Diana Spencer in 1981, they once again used their own special design of decoration unique to Weatherby's, but also used a general issue decoration as well. Both these designs can be found on an abundance of items. They were commissioned by the officers and crew of the Royal Yacht Britannia, to produce a special plate commemorating the honeymoon cruise, this was a limited edition of 500.

Another unusual Royal Commemorative was produced in 1983 to celebrate the Royal visit to the Caymen Islands, by Queen Elizabeth II and Prince Philip, once again this is a plate with a gold and red border. In fact they seem to have produced quite a few giftware items for the Caymen Islands. There is also, amongst the Weatherby Collection a mug to commemorate the Commonwealth Games held in Edinburgh, featuring Her Majesty the Queen in another especially commissioned design.

OTHER COMMEMORATIVES

Apart from the Royal connection, there are many other types of commemorative wares. We have a Green Howards mug, commemorating their centenary 1875–1975, and you will notice a plate with the same design on the Weatherby Giftware leaflet. On the same leaflet is a plate commemorating the Croydon Charter Centenary 1883–1983, with an impressive shield. In the Weatherby showrooms we found a plate depicting Nelson in the centre and a border showing the battles he fought, underneath the shield at the top of the plate is written 'The Death of Nelson'.

Amongst our own collection we have a colourful red and white plate produced for the British Amateur Athletic Board, European Cup in 1983, and in the Weatherby Collection we found a plate for the Royal National Life-Boat Institution, Lord Mayor of Manchester's Appeal, this was not dated.

BADGED WARE

Weatherby's are understandably proud of the quantity and diversity of the badged ware they produce. This is general use crockery supplied to restaurants, nightclubs, theatre bars, private clubs, regiments, universities and colleges. Mr. Jonathan Weatherby has very kindly supplied us with a selection of interesting badges, and these are reproduced on page 64. Amongst them are The Bath Club; Atheneum Club; City of London Club; The Reform Club; Carlton Club; The Butlers Wharf, Chop House; The Cavalry and Guards Club; Royal Engineers, WOs & Sgts Mess, Chattenden; Royal Army Ordinance Corp; South Notts Hussars; St. Edmund Hall, Oxford University; Pembroke College.

The badge shown for the GWR Refreshment Department, Swindon, is a reproduction, the original ceased to be used after nationalisation of the railways took place. This was probably reproduced for the Railway Museum at Swindon.

Although the above examples are relatively recent, the badged ware goes back many years, and we found a striking blue badge for the Leicester City Mental Hospital in the Weatherby Collection, (similar to the one for the Leicester Isolation Hospital shown on page 64), in our own collection we have a plate with the badge Wesleyan Methodist Church, Fearby. There are many pre-war examples, and amongst these are The Three Tuns Hotel, Dorking; Wellington College; The Green Man, Catford; St. Georges Hotel, Cliftonville; The Holborn Restaurant; P. Cullen & Sons. Our favourite is The Kiwi Refreshment Rooms this includes a picture of a Kiwi, which conjures up a typical 1930's tearoom somewhere in New Zealand.

◄ Selection of commemoratives from 1935 to 1981, from the Weatherby Collection.

Centre photograph from the Weatherby Collection other photographs by Tony and Jackie Chew.

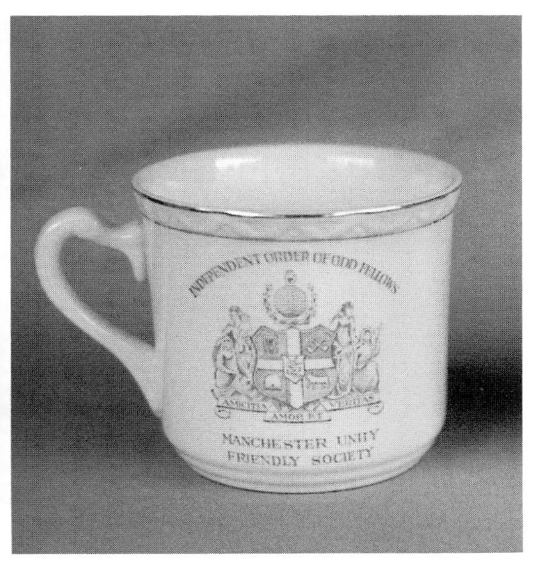

▲ From the collection of and photographed
▼▼by Tony and Jackie Chew.

▲ Photograph by Jonathan Weatherby.

▼ A limited edition of 500 plates were commissioned by the officers and crew of The Royal Yacht Britannia in 1981.

▼ 'The Death of Nelson'.

▲ Produced during the 1920's.

◀ Early plant pot and stand made by Mr. J.H. Weatherby senior.

▼ Leaflets showing colour patterns available in the 1920's.

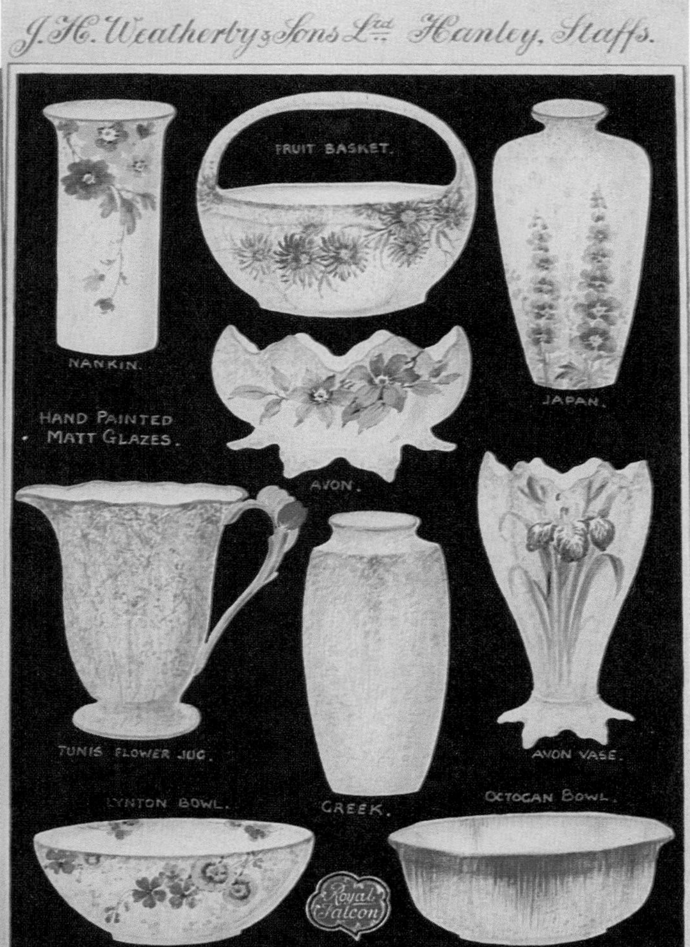

◄ Produced during the 1920's.

► Some of the colourful patterns produced during the mid-1920's and early 1930's.

▲ Produced during the early to mid-1930's.

▼ These designs were registered in the mid-1930s.

▲ Woodpecker Ware flower jug c1934 pattern number 5177.

▲ Jug number 4, pattern number 5642, 1930's.

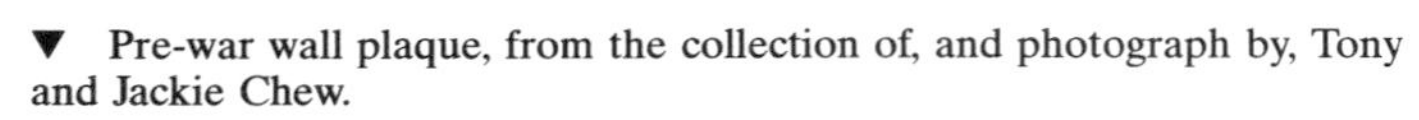

▼ Pre-war wall plaque, from the collection of, and photograph by, Tony and Jackie Chew.

▼ Vase number 71, Moongate pattern, c1935.

▲ Cake stand, pattern 6563, early 1950's, from the collection of, and photograph by, Tony and Jackie Chew.

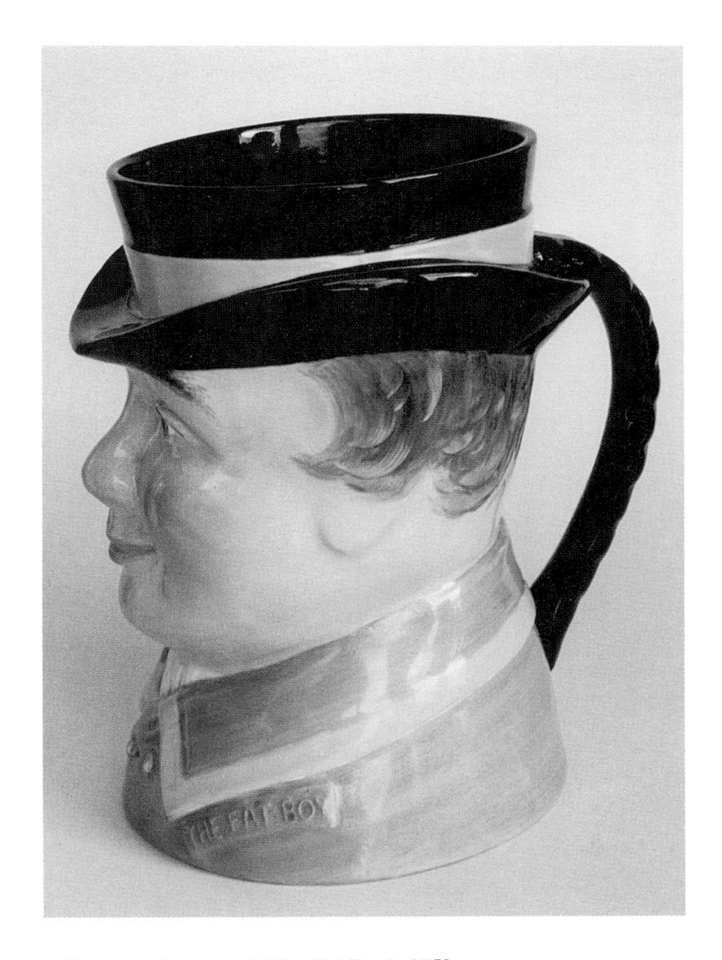

▲ Character jug named 'The Fat Boy' c1950.

▼ From left: Honies, pattern 7096 Rosa c1956, Delphine range, and pattern 7918 June Ware, both c1960.

Leaflets showing wares available during the 1960's.

▲ Zookie number 36
Nosey Mouse.

▲ Zookie number 34
Ass sitting.

▲ Zookie number 31
Rabbit with flower.

◀ Hen mustard pot.

▶ Zookie number 13
Zebra.

◀ Five
Weatherby
Dwarfs.

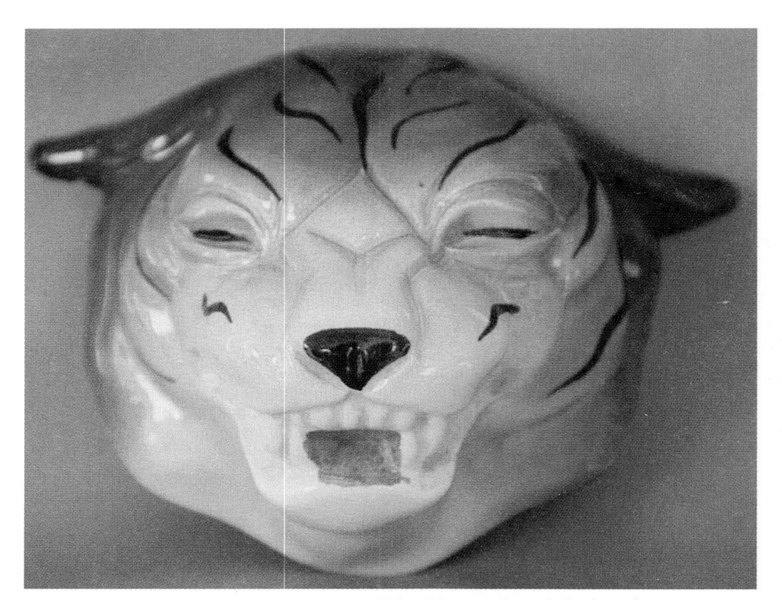

▲ A rare Tiger Zodieplac 4½″ high 5¾″ wide, produced during the 1960's. From the collection of Geoff Lynch.

▼ A 1990's leaflet showing a selection of commemorative and giftware available.

▼ A selection of the colourful backstamps.

1891–1892

c1925

c1929–1935

1934–1949

1936–1950

1970+

1963+

CHAPTER SIX

WEATHERBY BACKSTAMPS

▲ 1891–1892.

▲ 1893–1925.

▲ 1893–1925.

All single colours, the pattern name is above the flag.

▲ The Falcona Ware name was used from 1914–1925.

▲ c1920. Usually green.

▲ c1925. Note the 'A' has now been removed from 'FALCONA'. Usually green.

▲ c1926–1930 back stamp usually seen on Lustre Ware. Note pattern number 4053. Black or red.

▲ 1940–1945. The 'B' indicates it was a wartime product. Green.

▲ c1949. Pattern number 6561. Brown.

▲ c1949. Wild Duck pattern. Brown.

▲ 1956–1970. Used on animals and figures, often without Hanley. Green or black.

▲ 'Gonks' back stamp c1960–1970. Gold.

▲ A different style of pattern number dating c1960. Gold.

▲ 4/63 indicates this item was made in April 1963. Green.

▲ Much used by other companies. Do not use as sole identification. Found on 1950's and 1960's products. Black or green.

MADE EXCLUSIVELY
FOR THE
GREEN HOWARDS

H M S VICTORY
made exclusively for
H.M.S. Victory Souvenir Shop
by
J.H.Weatherby & Sons Ltd
Falcon Pottery
Hanley
England

From the 1970's Weatherbys produced many exclusive lines, and continue to do so.

Please note: There is a wide range of Weatherby back stamps to be found, consequently it is possible they come in colours other than those mentioned.

▲ Red White and Blue Gift Ware stamp used from 1970.

▲ Ironstone included from late 1970's.

▲ Falconite first used c1983. Green.

▲▼ These are just a few of the many back stamps now produced for the Giftware, Souvenir, and Hotel Ware ranges. No doubt you will find many others.

CHAPTER SEVEN
ZOOKIES, OTHER ANIMALS AND FIGURES

Produced during the 1950's and 1960's

ZOOKIES

Zookies, '***44 Different lighthearted Pottery Animal Figures with Comical Expressions, colourfully hand decorated and individually boxed in Presentation Cartons***' were produced from 1957 until the early 1970's. These are now collectors' items, and very much sought after. They were introduced gradually, between 1956 and 1962, the earlier numbers 1–28 are quite well illustrated on Weatherby advertising leaflets, but the later editions, numbers 29 – 44 have not been illustrated. (See Zookie Register on page 91). It is not known if they were all produced, but we, along with other collectors have managed to find a few which seem to fit in with the names we have found on Weatherby sales sheets, we show photographs of these on the following pages. Three of the Zookies have been found in two sizes, this fact has not been mentioned on any official literature, so it is possible others were also in two sizes.

The Zookie name seems particularly apt for these amusing animals, and they are enormous fun to collect. Rabbit, number five, with red or green coat is probably the most common, he was certainly the first one in our collection. They all have a particularly shiny glaze, almost a lustre finish, and are marked Weatherby on the base or the feet. (See back stamps on page 74). The majority of Zookies have cheerful features, large eyes and are very appealing.

BEASTIES

Beasties, what a wonderful name, were introduced about 1958 and produced for about five years. They were a range of six Jurassic Age monsters, fortunately reduced in size to about six inches long. They were available in black, white or mottled green, (see Beasties Register on page 92). The Beasties in the advert on the following pages are the only ones we have seen, apart from a few unglazed examples at the factory. They would appear to be extremely rare, and have yet to make an appearance at the Collectors' Fairs.

LIFE-LIKE ANIMALS

Life-Like Animals, '***A Series of animals, each one hand decorated in natural permanent under the glaze colours***'. This range was introduced in the early 1960's for about five years, and is a small range of 13 animals. (See Life Like Register on page 91). There aren't any particular distinguishing features to this range, so consequently are difficult to recognise amongst the many other models issued by other potteries. They are marked Weatherby on the base or feet. (See back stamps on page 74).

SEA TWINKS

Sea Twinks are a bit of a mystery. The advertising leaflet (shown on page 79) is undated, and we have found no Sea Twink paperwork at the Weatherby factory. They appear in the Weatherby Collection including a boxed set, and we have to assume they were made during the 'Weatherby Novelty Period' (1950's and 1960's) when so many new ideas were forthcoming. They are small wall plaques, except for the seaweed and coral which are free standing, and coloured in soft pastel shades, presumably meant as bathroom decorations.

CHUCKLEHEADS

Chuckleheads were a childrens' range of three cups and saucers in the shape of animals, a pig, monkey and elephant. The designs are quite extraordinary and great fun, but look most cumbersome for little children to hold. They came in their own Chuckle Head box, and were produced for a few years in the early 1960's.

OTHER ANIMALS

Amongst the paper work at the Weatherby factory we came across some intriguing names, here are a few examples: 'Chunkies, Wistfuls, Zodieplacs, Dog and Donkey Zookie style, Large Dog, Middle Dog with ears, Dumpy Dog, Tiny Dog, Tall Rabbit with ears, Dumpy Rabbit long ears'. We don't know for certain which animals these are, and no one at the factory can remember, but several collectors have made some interesting finds which are illustrated on the following pages.

The Weatherby Collection also contains various unnamed animals, some of which are illustrated on the following pages, but it is important for all collectors to be very open minded when looking for Weatherby animals, as we believe many are undocumented. Most of these animals are white glazed, with black eyes nose and mouth, sometimes a satin finish has been used. Recently a collector found a Dumpy Dog fawn coloured with only eyes and nose in black.

DWARFS

Five dwarfs have been found by ourselves and other collectors. They are very much in the mould of Snow White's seven friends but two seem to be missing. A number of collectors have the five dwarfs, so although they are not easy to find, they are not particularly rare. We have found no paperwork, adverts, or Pottery Gazette advertisements about this range and no one at the factory had any information. Mrs. Dorothy Gallagher who was employed at the factory for many years can remember painting them. She didn't think they were part of the seven dwarfs, but were of another different series. We found a few in the Weatherby Collection in white glaze, but unfortunately cannot find any more information about these colourful little fellows. (See pages 71 and 87).

ALICE IN WONDERLAND

It was planned to produce a range of Alice in Wonderland characters in 1958, according to the Pottery Gazette. We have seen an advertising leaflet for these, and there are prices quoted for them in the price lists. Then the Disney Corporation who had commissioned them, withdrew the contract, and they were not put into production. However, just for interest, and in case some did come on the market, we have included the group in a photograph on page 87.

All the above animals or figures are now eagerly collected, and are bound to escalate in price as they were produced for such a short time. We would be very pleased to hear from collectors of any other Weatherby Novelties they have found.

Stop Press: Shirley Robson has recently found an unusual wall plaque, the silhouette of a lady's head, in a cream glaze, with a rim on the back, and marked Weatherby, England. (See page 87).

DRINKING IS CHILD'S PLAY WITH . . .
Chuckleheads
Registration applied for
Decorated in hygienic under-glaze colours—Enhance your counter with this attractive point of sale pack
J. H. WEATHERBY & SONS LIMITED
FALCON POTTERY · HANLEY · STAFFORDSHIRE
DRINKING IS CHILDS PLAY WITH
Chuckleheads
BY
Weatherby
HANLEY ENGLAND
Chuckleheads

▲ Chucklehead cups and saucers, produced for a few years during the early 1960's.

◄ Rudy (baby dachshund) number 38, 4″ long.

Reprinted from the POTTERY GAZETTE AND GLASS TRADE REVIEW, *July*, 1958.

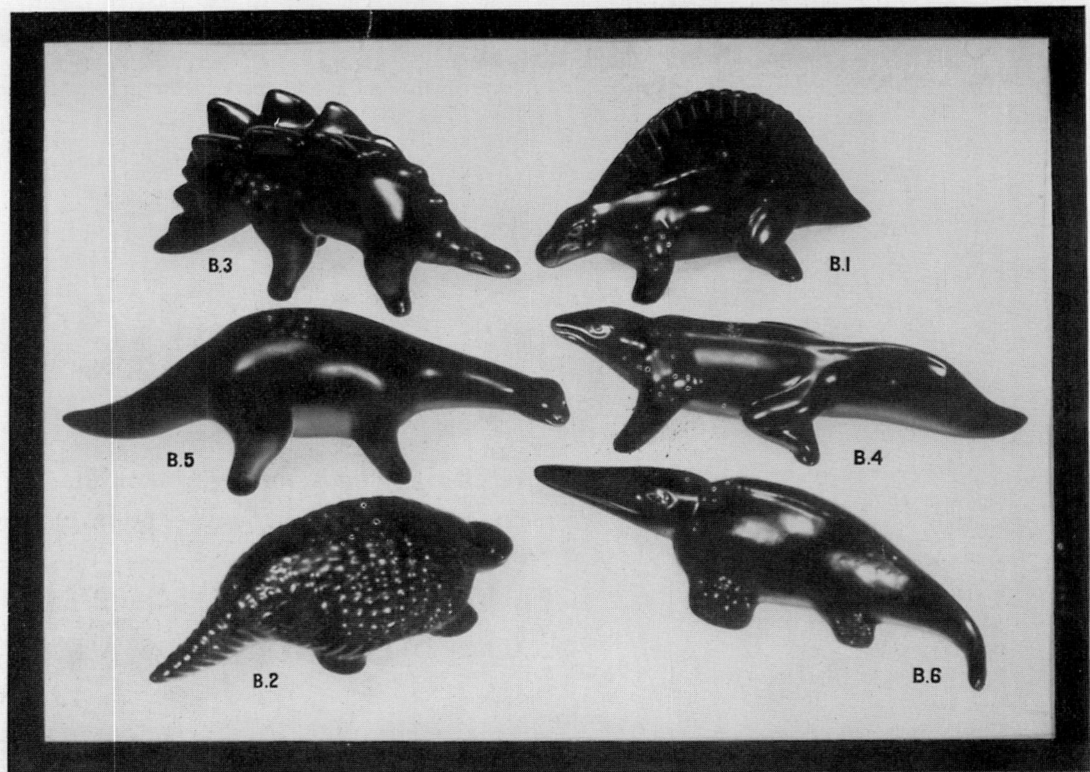

Our ancestor on the left is much happier about these Beasties than he was in the Jurassic Age. Now they are about 6 inches long and from two to five inches in height.
You also can be happy about " Beasties." Beautifully made and in presentation boxes, this series of six is a sure sales getter. They retail around 9/6 and can be bought either in black as above, or in white.
Send your trial order now.

J. H. WEATHERBY & SONS LTD

FALCON POTTERY · HANLEY · STAFFS

Agents : LONDON: A. E. Jones, 321 High Holborn, London, W.C.I. AUSTRALIA: W. Forester & Co. (Pty.) Ltd., 232, Castlereagh Street, Sydney. SOUTH AFRICA: Bradford-Campbell & Co., C.T.C. Buildings, Plein Street, Capetown. NEW ZEALAND: D. L. Bade & Co. Ltd., 153, Featherston Street, Wellington, C.I. ARGENTINA: Murray Lea & Co., Rivadavia, 1142, Buenos Aires. CUBA: Miguel Dota, Ep. 427, Santiago de Cuba. BRITISH WEST INDIES: Alex Russell & Co., Bridgetown, Barbados. BRITISH GUIANA: Alex Russell & Co., Georgetown, Demerara.

Beasties from the Jurassic Age, produced from the late 1950's for a few years, 2–5″ high 6″ long.

Introducing
Sea Twinks
by Weatherby
Produced in soft greens, greys and pastel pinks on off-white grounds, these registered designs of marine fauna and flora meet the ever-increasing interest in attractive wall decoration for all rooms. Easily affixed and as easily removed, Sea Twinks will find a ready sale among your discerning clientele.
Sea Twinks are boxed both separately and collectively.
Sea Twinks
by Weatherby
J. H. WEATHERBY & SONS LIMITED
FALCON POTTERY · HANLEY · STAFFS
AGENTS
LONDON: A. E. Jones, 321 High Holborn, London, W.C.1.
AUSTRALIA: W. Forester & Co. (Pty.) Ltd., 232, Castlereagh Street, Sydney.
SOUTH AFRICA: Bradford-Campbell & Co., C.T.C. Buildings, Plein Street, Capetown.
NEW ZEALAND: D. L. Bade & Co. Ltd., 153, Featherston Street, Wellington, C.1.
N. RHODESIA: A. R. McEwan, 12, Mutual Building, Coronation Square, Kitwe.
ARGENTINA: Murray Lea & Co., Rivadavia, 1142, Buenos Aires.
CUBA: Miguel Dota, Ep. 427, Santiago de Cuba.
BRITISH WEST INDIES: Alec Russell & Co., Bridgetown, Barbados.
BRITISH GUIANA: Alec Russell & Co., Georgetown, Demerara.

Sea Twinks, probably produced during the 1950's and 1960's, decorated in pastel colours.

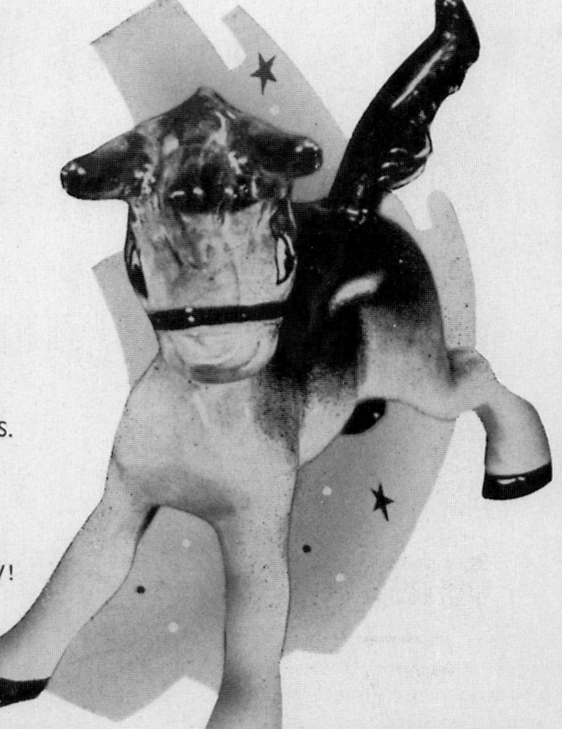

These attractive animal caricatures will capture the hearts of your customers at sight.
Gay and bright, they add charm and colour to every room. People who buy one, buy another . . . and another and buy them for their friends too!
Those illustrated are some of the ZOOKIES. Others are the baby tiger, the seal, the lamb, the penguin (very stylish) and the crocodile (very Nile-ish). Other fascinating ZOOKIES are in production. Make your selection - NOW!

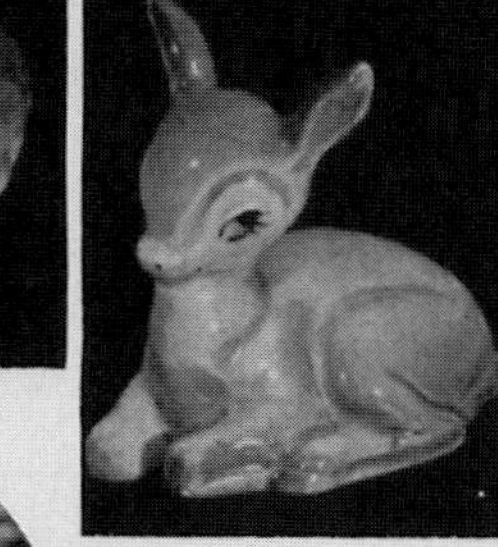

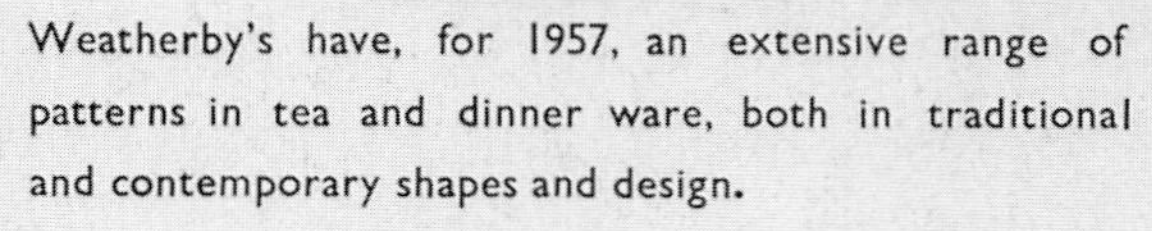

Weatherby's have, for 1957, an extensive range of patterns in tea and dinner ware, both in traditional and contemporary shapes and design.
Fancies are, as ever, a Weatherby speciality.

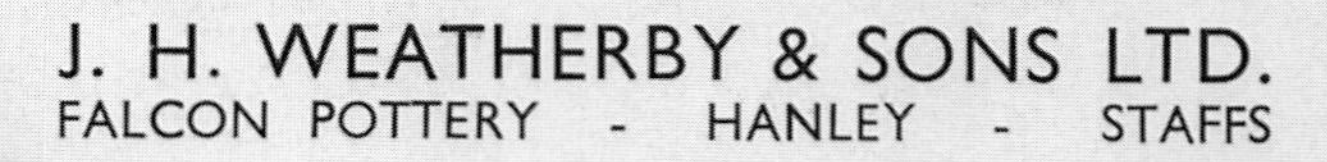

The first series of Zookies were introduced towards the end of 1956.

The friendliest animals (and birds) in Pottery Creation
Guaranteed House Trained.

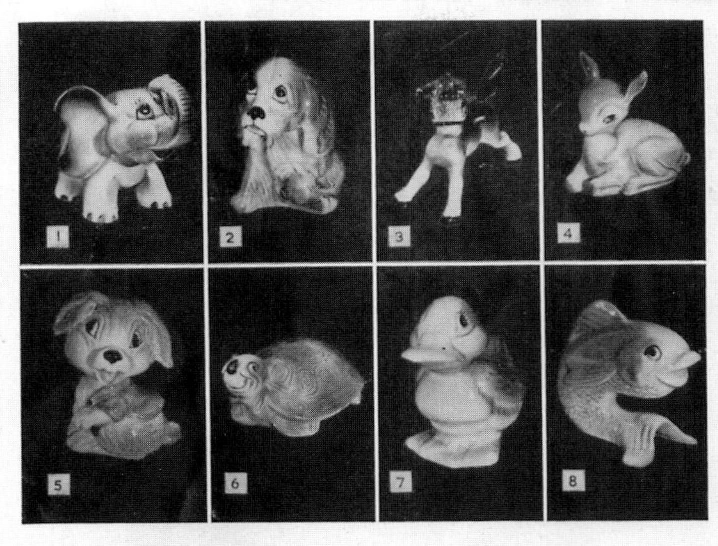

1. ELEPHANT
2. DOG
3. HORSE
4. FAWN
5. RABBIT
6. TORTOISE
7. DUCK
8. FISH

ZOOKIES
by Weatherby

9. LAMB
10. CROCODILE
11. PENGUIN
12. DUCK
13. ZEBRA
14. SEAL
15. TIGER CUB
16. KITTEN & BALL

J. H. WEATHERBY & SONS LIMITED ***FALCON POTTERY, HANLEY, STAFFS***

AGENTS

A. E. Jones, 321 High Holborn, London, W.C.1.
W. Forester & Co. (Pty) Ltd., 232, Castlereagh Street, Sydney.
Bradford-Campbell & Co., C.T.C. Buildings, Plein Street, Cape Town.
D. L. Bade & Co. Ltd., 153, Featherston Street, Wellington. C.1.

ARGENTINA: Murray, Lea & Co., Rivadavia 1142, Buenos Aires.
CUBA: Miguel Dota Ap. 427, Santiago de Cuba.
BRITISH WEST INDIES: Alec Russell & Co., Bridgetown, Barbados.
BRITISH GUIANA: Alec Russell & Co., Georgetown, Demerara.

In February 1957, another eight Zookies came on to the market, numbers nine to sixteen.

Zookies were proving to be very popular and as a result another eight animals, numbers seventeen to twenty-four, appeared in 1958.

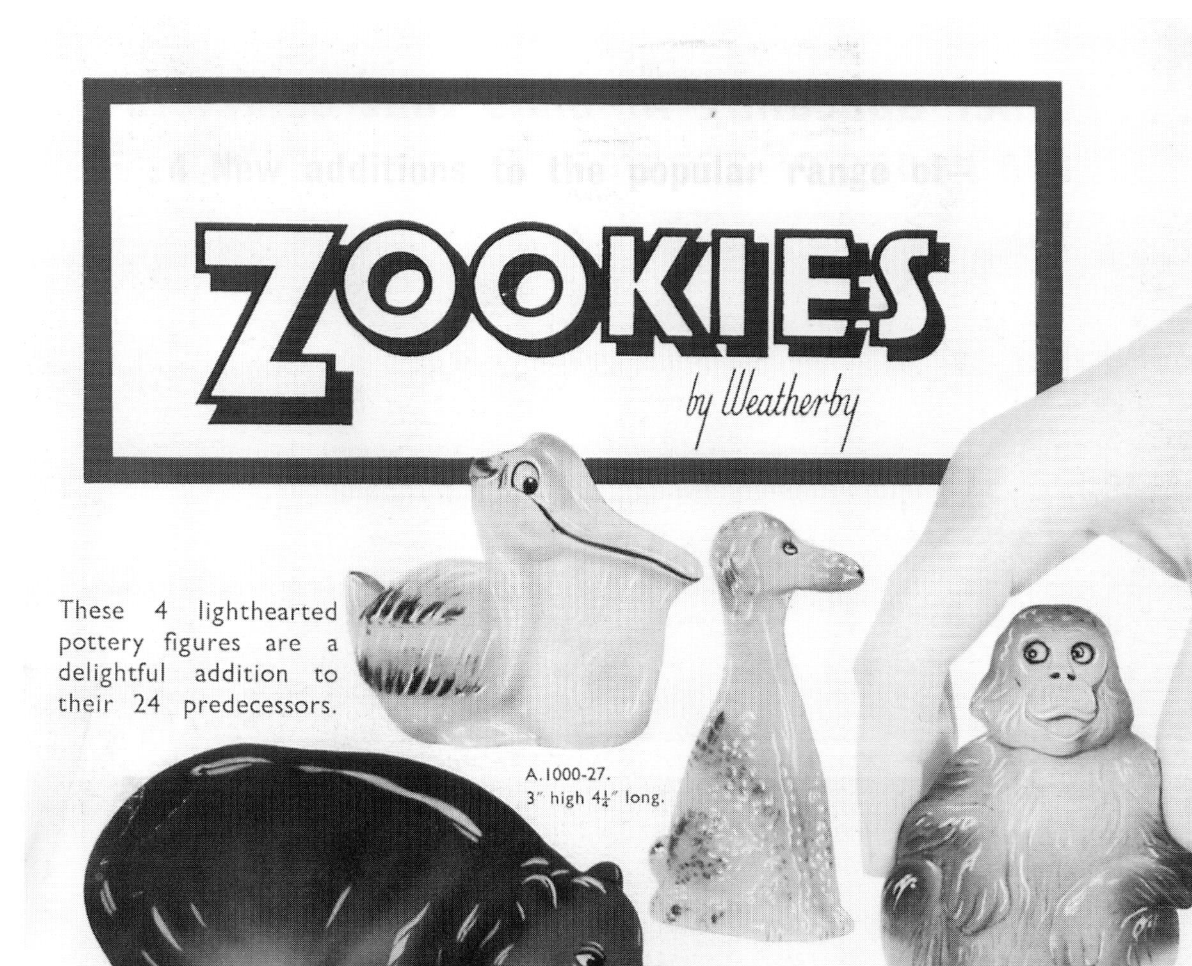

ZOOKIES
by Weatherby
These 4 lighthearted pottery figures are a delightful addition to their 24 predecessors.

A.1000-27.
3" high 4¼" long.

A.1000-25. 4" high.

A.1000-28. 5½" long x 3" high.

A.1000-26. 4" high.

A.1000-22. 2" high 5" long.

A.1000-3. $3\frac{13}{16}$" high.

A.1000-2. 3¼" high.

A.1000-24. 4½" high.

J. H. WEATHERBY & SONS LTD

FALCON POTTERY, HANLEY, STAFFS

AGENTS

A. E. Jones (Hotel Ware), 321 High Holborn, London, W.C.1
J. H. Chignall & Co. (other lines), 6/8 Amwell St., London, E.C.1
W. Forester & Co. (Pty) Ltd., Castlereagh Street, Sydney.
Bradford-Campbell & Co., C.T.C. Buildings, Plein St., Capetown.
D. L. Bade & Co. Ltd., 153 Featherston St., Wellington, C.1
Murray, Lea & Co., Rivadavia 1142, Buenos Aires, Argentina.
Migual Dota, Ep. 427 Santiago de Cuba.
Alex Russell & Co., Bridgetown, Barbados.
Alex Russell & Co., Georgetown, Demerara, British Guiana.

In 1959 four more Zookies were designed, bringing the total to twenty-eight.

....other appealing Animals that complete the range of zookies...

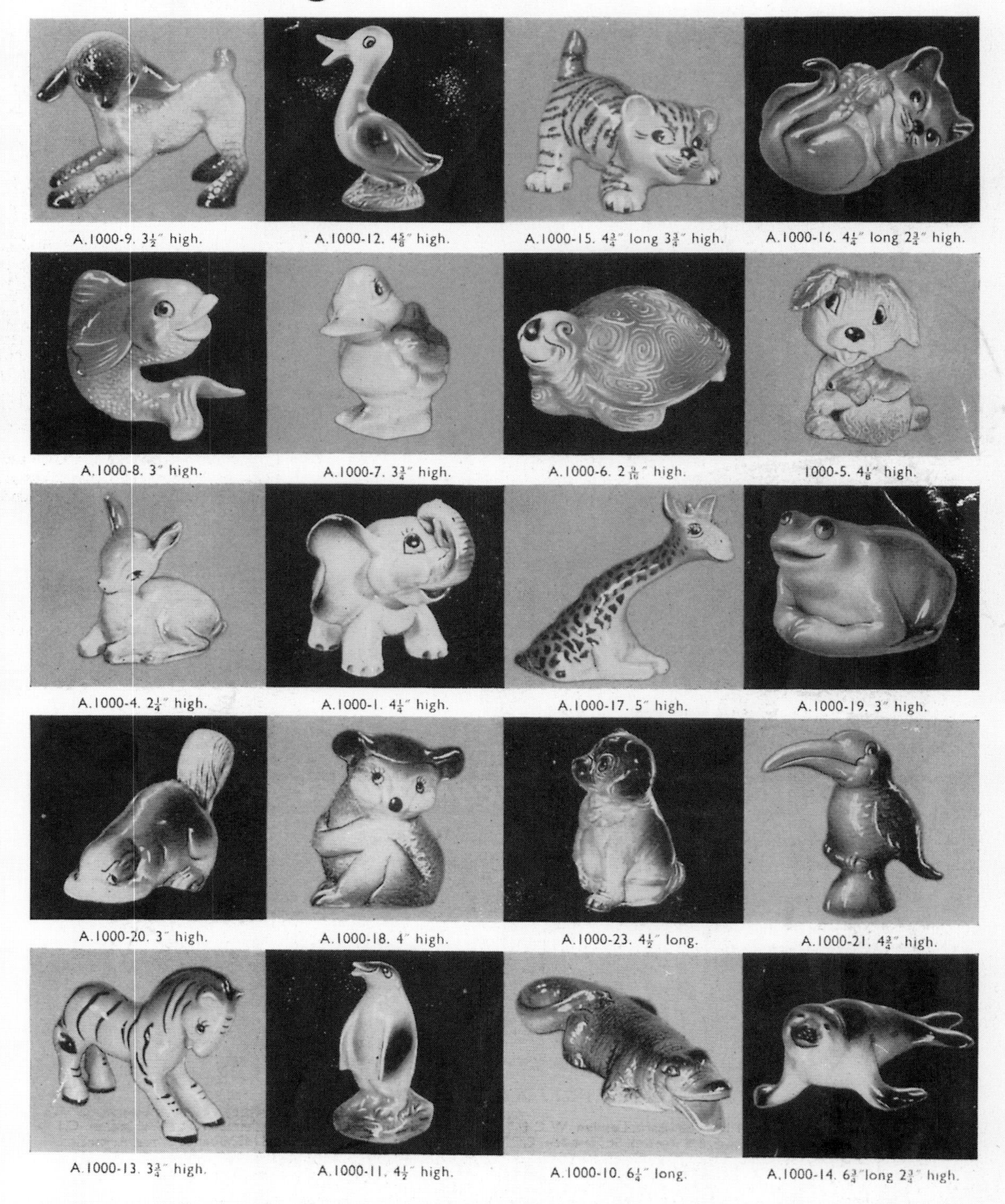

Leaflet showing twenty Zookies, giving the numbers and the heights. Production probably ceased towards the end of the 1960's.

▲ This delightful chap is probably Zookie number 34, he was found by Shirley Robson and has joined her ever growing collection. He is 4½″ high and can be seen in colour on page 71.

◀ This handsome dog also belongs to Shirley Robson, he looks very much like Tramp, but may be number 39, Scruff 5½″ high.

▼ Three more 'lost' Zookies from the last series, we think they are number 29 Mule 5½″ high, number 40 Sitting Elephant 4¾″ high, and number 31 Rabbit with Flower 3¾″ high.

◀ We can't find a name for the dog on the left, he is 3¼" high and 4½" long, we call him 'Silly Pup', the dog on the right is very similar to Boxer Pup number 23. It is possible he was redesigned.

▶ We would say, without a doubt, this is number 36 Nosey Mouse 3½" high. Collected and photographed by Tony and Jackie Chew. Can be seen in colour on page 71.

▼ The large duck is very similar to Zookie number 12, 4⅝" high, but in fact he is 6½" high, and has quite different colouring. Photographed by and from the collection of John and Pauline Thake.

▼ ▶ Elephant number 1 was also made in two sizes, from the collection of Shirley Robson.

▲ The large penguin is 8″ high, a larger version of number 11 4½″ high, the kangaroo is 8″ high (we wondered if he could be number 37 Skip). All from the Weatherby Collection.

▲ The set of Alice in Wonderland characters which apparently never went into production. All from the Weatherby Collection.

▼ Five Weatherby dwarfs, can also be seen in colour on page 71.

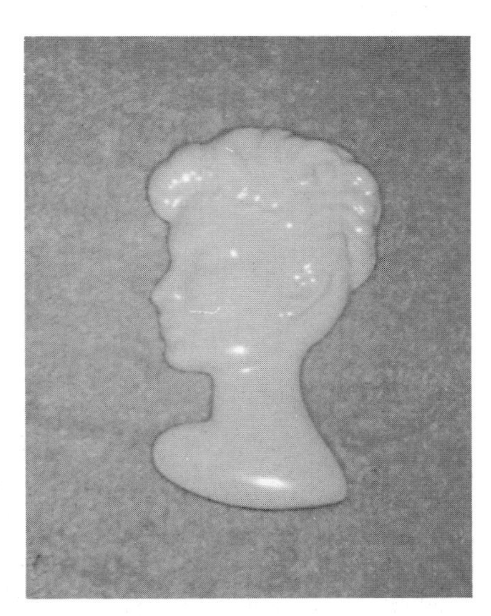

▲ Head wall plaque 6¼″ high 3¾″ wide. From the collection of Shirley Robson.

◀ Four more animals found in the Weatherby Collection, the Mule is 4½″ high, the Cat is 3½″ high, the Hare is 2″ high and 5″ long (he may be Zookie number 33) and Scottie is 2″ high.

▶ Monkey 2½″ high and Pig 2¼″ high, both white glazed. There is also a small owl seen in the Weatherby Collection.

◀ Tiny Mouse 2½″ high, Cheshire Cat 4″ high, Tiny Elephant 2½″ high and number 36 Nosey Mouse 3½″ high, all white glaze and from the Weatherby Collection.

White matt rabbit $6\frac{1}{2}''$ high from the collection
f Shirley Robson.

▲ Dumpy dog white matt is $5\frac{1}{2}''$ high $6\frac{1}{2}''$ long, there is a small version which is $3''$ high. From the collection of and photographed by Shirley Robson.

▼ Small horse from the Life Like Animals range $5\frac{1}{4}''$ high.

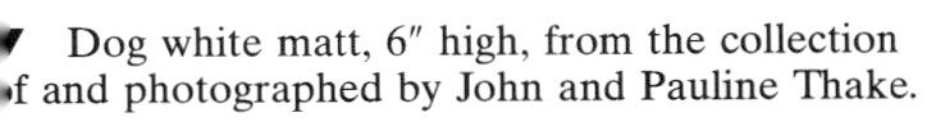

▼ Dog white matt, $6''$ high, from the collection
f and photographed by John and Pauline Thake.

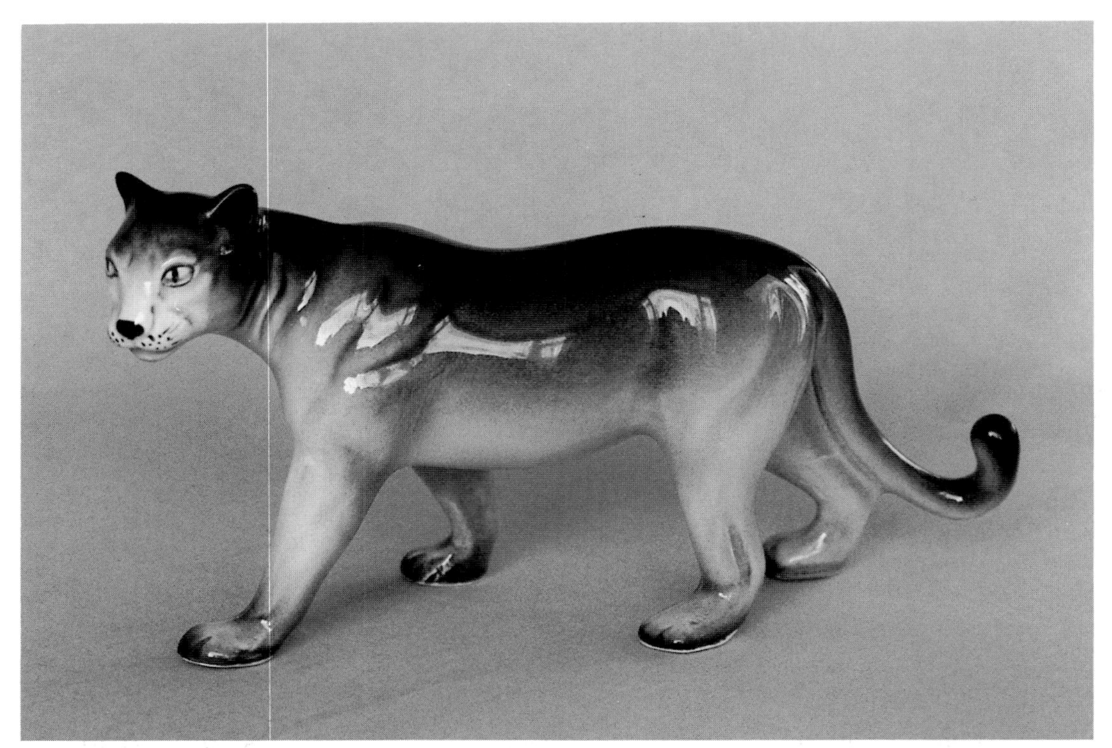

▲ Panther from the Life Like Animals range 4″ high 7$\frac{3}{4}$″ long. From the collection of and photographed by Tony and Jackie Chew.

◀ Medium size elephant from the Life Like Animals range 5″ high 6$\frac{1}{2}$″ long.

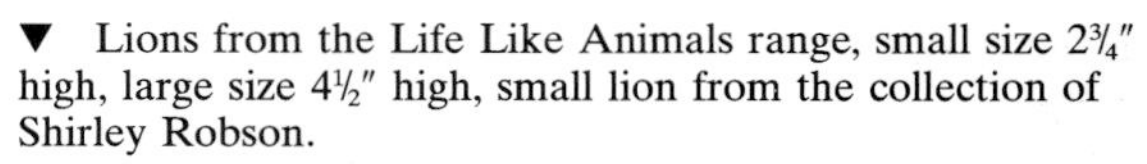

▼ Lions from the Life Like Animals range, small size 2$\frac{3}{4}$″ high, large size 4$\frac{1}{2}$″ high, small lion from the collection of Shirley Robson.

CHAPTER EIGHT

REGISTERS

ZOOKIE ANIMALS

Although the Weatherby factory gave numbers to Zookies these were for reference purposes only, and were not impressed on the bases. The prefix A-1000 was used at first, but this was eventually discontinued. Two sizes of some Zookies have been found, and these have also been noted. Production of all Zookies had ceased by 1970.

Ref No.	*Description*	*Size*	*Page number*
December 1956			
1	Elephant standing	4¼″h	80, 81, 84
*	Elephant standing	4″h	86
2	Dog Spaniel	3¼″h	80, 81, 83
3	Horse	4″h	80, 81, 83
4	Fawn	2¼″h	80, 81, 84
5	Rabbit red coat	4⅛″h	80, 81, 84
5	Rabbit green coat	4⅛″h	80, 81, 84
6	Tortoise	2⅜″h	80, 81, 84
7	Duck (dumpy)	3¾″h	80, 81, 84
8	Fish	3″h	80, 81, 84
9	Lamb standing	3½″h	81, 84
February 1957			
10	Crocodile	6¼″l	81, 84
11	Penguin	4½″h	81, 84
*	Penguin	8″h	87
12	Duck (tall)	4⅝″h	81, 84
*	Duck (tall)	6½″h	86
13	Zebra	3¾″h	71, 81, 84
14	Seal	2¾″h 6¾″l	81, 84
15	Tiger cub	2¾″h 4¾″l	81, 84
16	Kitten and ball	2¾″h 2¼″l	81, 84
1958			
17	Giraffe sitting	5″h	82, 84
18	Koala bear	4″h	82, 84
19	Frog	3″h	82, 84
20	Skunk	3″h	82, 84
21	Toucan	4¾″h	82, 84
22	Dachshund standing	2″h 5″l	82, 83
23	Boxer pup sitting	4½″l	82, 84
24	Camel standing	4½″h	82, 83
1959			
25	Poodle sitting	4″h	83
26	Monkey sitting	4″h	83
27	Pelican	3″h 4¼″l	83
28	Hippo standing	3″h 5½″l	83

The following Zookies were in the factory price lists but not officially illustrated. We have tried to identify them but our assumptions may not be correct, we cannot be sure they were all produced.

1961			
29	Mule sitting	5½″h	85
30	Dog (Butch)		
31	Rabbit with flower	3¾″h	71, 85
32	Cat and mouse		
33	Hare (sandwich)	2″h 5″l	88
34	Ass sitting	4¼″h	71, 85
35	Singing cats		
36	Nosey Mouse	3½″h	71, 86, 88
37	Skip	8″h	87
38	Rudy (baby dachshund)		77
1962			
39	Dog (Scruff)	5½″h	85
40	Sitting elephant	4¾″h	85
41	Deer		
42	Squirrel		
43	Pekinese		
44	Sitting lamb		

*INDICATES – NO REFERENCE NUMBER KNOWN

LIFE-LIKE ANIMALS

A series of animals each one hand decorated in natural permanent under the glaze colours. The Shetland pony and tiger were made for a short period only, the others had ceased by 1970.

1960		*Page*
Shetland pony		
Clydesdale horse	6¾″h 8¼″l	70
Clydesdale foal	5½″h 5″l	70, 89
Elephant l/s	6¼″h 7½″l	70
Elephant m/s	5″h 6½″l	70, 90
Elephant s/s	2¼″h 3½″l	70
Panther	4″h 7¾″l	70, 90
Polar bear l/s	3½″h 5″l	70
Polar bear	1¼″h 2″l	70
Lion l/s	4½″h	90
Lion s/s	2¾″h 6¾″l	90
Tiger	3″h	
Hunter	5″h	

BEASTIES

A pre-historic animal series, available in black, white or mottled green. They were given factory reference numbers, which were not impressed on the bases. Production had ceased by 1970. Illustrated on page 78.

1958

B1	Permian reptile	3½″h 6″l
B2	Gliptodont	2″h 5″l
B3	Stegosaurus	3½″h 6″l
B4	Giant Lizard	1¾″h 6¾″l
B5	Apatosaurus	2½″h 7″l
B6	Tyannosaurus	2″h 7″l

OTHER ANIMALS

These names have been taken from price lists dated 1962, they have been given factory reference numbers.

1 Large dog
2 Middle dog with ears
3 Dumpy dog
4 Dumpy rabbit long ears l/s
5 Dumpy rabbit long ears s/s
6 Tall rabbit with ears
7 Tiny dog

These descriptions were taken from a price list c1960

Chunkies one dog one cat in box

Wistfuls one per box

Dog and donkey one per box green mottled

Dog and donkey Zookie style

Wall heads done as Zookie style

Krazy cats

Zodieplacs

VASES, FLOWER JUGS, PLANT POTS, DISHES AND BOWLS

The Weatherby factory started to impress numbers on their ranges during the 1930's, some of the vases incorporated into this list had been given shape names earlier. The production of vases ceased during the 1970's apart from one or two small ranges.

c1930–1940 (Some had been produced earlier and given shape names).

Number	*Description*	*Size*	*Page number*
1	Vase ribbed	9″h	39
2	Vase ribbed	7″h	39
3	F/Jug ribbed sim to 4/56	8″h	39
4	F/Jug ribbed sim to 3/56	7″h	39, 68
5	Vase plain sim to 14	8½″h	39
6	F/Jug ribbed (diagonal)	10″h	39
7	Vase ribbed ornamental handles	10″h	39
8	Vase embossed palm trees	9″h	39
9	Oval tray ribbed	11½″l	39
10	Posy bowl	6″dia	39
11	Vase plain	10″h	39, 65
12	Vase six-sided	9¾″h	39
13	Bud vase sim to 18	8″h	39
14	Vase plain sim to 5	9¾″h	39
15	Vase plain	7″h	40
16	Vase six-sided	10″h	40
17	Vase six-sided	9″h	40
18	Bud vase sim to 13	8½″h	40
19	Vase plain sim to 20	7″h	40
20	Vase plain sim to 19	5½″h	40
21	Vase straight sides	12″h	40
22	Vase straight sides	10″h	40
23	Vase straight sides	8″h	40, 65
24	Vase straight sides (21,22,23,24 all sim)	6¾″h	40
25	Vase six-sided	7″h	40
26	Candle holder	2½″h	40
27	Vase plain	6½″h	40
28	Slop bowl	3½″h	40
29	Bowl six-sided	9″dia	40
30	Bowl six-sided	8″dia	40
31	Bowl six-sided (29,30,31 all sim)	7½″d	40
32	Vase plain sim to 36	5¾″h	40
33	Bowl round	9½″dia	40
34	Bowl round	8½″dia	40, 65
35	Bowl round (33,34,35 all sim)	7½″dia	40
36	Vase plain sim to 32	4½″h	41
37	Plant pot plain	7½″h	41
38	Bowl round	9″dia	41
39	Bowl round	8″dia	41
40	Bowl round	7¼″dia	41
43	Basket with handle	8″l	41, 65
44	Vase scalloped edges (to match 45 and 46)	8″h	41, 65
45	Bowl scalloped edges	8″dia	41, 65
46	Bowl scalloped edges (45,46 sim)	10″dia	41
47	F/Jug ribbed with ornamental handles	7¾″h	41
48	Vase plain sim to 49	7″h	41
49	Vase plain sim to 48	5″h	41
50	Vase plain sim to 51	5¾″h	41
51	Vase plain sim to 50	4½″h	41
52	Plant pot six sided	8¼″h	41
53	Plant pot six sided	7¾″h	41
54	Plant pot six sided (52,53,54 all sim)	7″h	41
55	Vase plain	4½″h	42
56	Jug ribbed sim to 3/4	6½″h	42
57	Bowl scroll handles embossed 'paving'	7½″l	42
58	F/Jug ribbed Deco style	10″h	42
59	Vase fluted, embossed	15″h	42
60	F/Jug fluted top/base centre plain Deco style	14″h	42
61	F/Jug ribbed Deco style	10½″h	42
62	'Odeon' style vase embossed face	10″h	42
63	F/Jug ribbed	9¼″h	42
64	Sandwich tray Deco rays	9½″l	42
65	Plate triangular also used with chrome handle	10″l	42, 46

66	F/Jug ribbed Deco style	10¾"h	42
67	Vase side 'flashes'	10¼"h	42, 45
68	F/Jug ribbed Deco style	7¼"h	43
69	F/Jug ribbed Deco style	7"h	43
70	F/Jug Deco rays	9"h	43
71	F/Jug 'Moongate'	7"h	43, 68
72	Vase ribbed matches 73	9"h	43
73	F/Jug ribbed matches 72	9"h	43
74	Vase mottled two handles	10"h	43
75	Vase six sided two handles	10¼"h	43
76	Vase straight sides two handles	9"h	43
77	F/Jug mottled	9¾"h	43

1938

78	Bowl scalloped edge	7"l	43
79	Bowl ribbed	10"l	43
80	F/Jug mottled	10¼"h	43
81	F/Jug ribbed	10¼"h	44
82	F/Jug angular Deco style	7½"h	44
83	F/Jug ribbed	9¾"h	44
84	F/Jug mottled	9½"h	44
85	Vase horizontal scallops	9"h	44
86	Vase horizontal scallops two handles	9¾"h	44
87	Jug ribbed band	5½"h	44
88	Vase	6½"h	44
89	Vase ribbed band	8¼"h	44
90	F/Jug embossed leaves and bark	10"h	44
91	Bowl scalloped top	9"dia	44
92	Bowl scalloped top	7"dia	44

We believe, from the paper work in our possession that the following numbers were first produced during the 1950's. Some were used for the Brownie Downing series in the 1960's.

First produced c1950–1960

1950

93	Log posy straight	5½"l	51
94	Vase	8"h	51, 65
95	F/Jug	10"h	51
96	F/Jug	10"h	51
97	Log posy curved	6½"l	51
98	F/Jug embossed flowers trellis effect	8¾"h	51
99	Tree trunk vase	3¾"h	51
100	Vase lop sided	5¾"h	51
101	Small posy	2¾"h	51
102	Wall vase	3¼"h	51
103	Shell posy	2¾"h	51

1958

104	Vase lop sided	4"h	51
105	Vase lop sided	5"h	51
106	Plant pot with bumps	4"h	51
107	Tray with bumps	7"l	51
108	Tray with bumps	6"l	51
109	Tray with bumps	6"l	51
110	Dish boat shape	6"l	51
111	F/Jug plain	6"h	51
112	Vase plain	6"h	51
113	Plant pot plain	3½"h	51
114	Plant pot plain	5½"h	51
115	Tray plain	6¾"l	51
116	Wall? Vase embossed	7"h	51
117	Wall? Vase embossed	7"h	51
121	Vase plain	8"h	49, 52
122	Vase plain	7¾"h	52
123	Wall vase plain l/s	6¼"h	52
123	Wall vase plain s/s	4¼"h	52
124	Vase round with 'spout'	4"h	52
125	Vase plain	6"h	52
127	Vase scroll top	6"h	52
128	Dish plain	8½"dia	52
129	Vase on foot plain	6¾"h	52
130	Vase plain	8"h	52
130	Vase round fluted	7"h	52
131	Vase plain	8¼"h	52
132	Vase plain	8¼"h	52
133	Vase plain	8¼"h	52
134	Goblet vase	4"h	52
135	F/Jug angular handle	7½"h	52

DECORATION/PATTERN NUMBERS

The earliest pattern book we found at the Weatherby factory was dated 1899, and started with pattern number 499, fortunately this gave us a reliable starting date. We found only three pre-war Registered (design) Numbers, and with the help of the Public Records Office, these were also dated, giving us the years 1903, 1934 and 1936. Occasionally we found a decoration number on a dated Weatherby price list, or advert, and we used these as a guide. The list below is the result of averaging out the gaps between known dates, and must be regarded as a guide rather than an accurate record.

DECORATION NUMBERS	APPROXIMATE DATE
499	2nd September 1899
1348–1392	c1903
1400–2500	c1904–1912
2612–3466	c1913–1920
3588–4685	c1921–1929
4808–5174	c1930–1933
5177	c1934
5370	c1936
5665–6153	c1937–1941
6424–6563	c1949–1953
7033–7918	c1955–1962
8221	c1964

We have not found any numbers beyond this date

Abbreviations used in this section.

h = height.	l = length.	dia = diameter.
sim = similar.	plain = not embossed.	F/Jug = flower jug.
l/s = large size.	m/s = medium size.	s/s = small size.

PLEASE NOTE ALL MEASUREMENTS IN THESE LISTS MUST BE CONSIDERED AS APPROXIMATE ONLY. (We have found measurements vary in the factory lists.)

PART TWO

TELEGRAPHIC ADDRESS:
"FALCON, LONGTON."

TELEPHONE:
LONGTON 3728.

DIRECTORS :
E. J. DENNIS
R. HULL

~~Proprietor~~
~~J. GRUNDY~~.

(LONGTON) LTD.
MANUFACTURER OF
EARTHENWARE TOILET WARE & FANCY GOODS.

Falcon Pottery,
WATERLOO STREET,

STAFFS. 19

Photo by W. Williamson, Longton

MR. T. LAWRENCE.

PREFACE TO PART TWO

Interest in Thomas Lawrence, Falcon Ware, has occurred because of the connection with Shaw & Copestake Ltd., (SylvaC). There are many collectors of SylvaC and enormous fascination in the products, which in turn has led to a growing interest in the early products of the Falcon Pottery. The connection came about due to the joining together, by marriage, of the two families, resulting in the eventual combining of the businesses.

The Thomas Lawrence pottery had its own individual style, and it is the pre-war and wartime years that are concentrated on in the following chapters. The inevitable influence of Shaw & Copestake after the war, resulted in similar products, and these later years have been covered in my two earlier books, The SylvaC Story and The SylvaC Companion. As there are also some notes on the early days they should be read in conjunction with this book, as I have endeavoured not to repeat information or photographs already published.

It was a task taken on with some reluctance, due to lack of material available. Despite strenuous efforts on my part, no pre-war catalogues or advertising brochures have been found, which is a great disadvantage when compiling a reference book! However, I unearthed some documents from the Shaw & Copestake factory, and Mick and Derry Collins also lent me material they had accumulated during their search for SylvaC. Jeanette Holdcroft, daughter of Reginald Thompson (Chief Designer), had a wonderful collection of original drawings, notebooks and photographs, left by her father. When the time came to start making some order out of my research notes, I was surprised at how much information I had eventually gathered.

As usual I have cajoled collectors into providing photographs, and many of these are reproduced in order to help with identification of Falcon Ware. Everyone has rallied round to help with this project, it really has been a combined effort, and my thanks go to everyone who has helped. There is still a lot to learn about the Thomas Lawrence company, and I hope readers will share any information they have with me so that I can eventually update the book. I take great pleasure in publishing the latest information about the Thomas Lawrence, Falcon Pottery.

CHAPTER ONE
HISTORY OF THE COMPANY

THOMAS LAWRENCE (LONGTON) LTD
Falcon Works
Waterloo Street
Longton
Stoke-on-Trent.

THOMAS LAWRENCE (born in 1862) founded his factory in Wharf Street, Stoke-on-Trent c1888, he moved in 1898 to the Falcon Pottery, Waterloo Street, Longton, (Waterloo Street has since been renamed Barford Street). The move to Waterloo Street was announced in the Pottery Gazette on May 2nd 1898:

"Thomas Lawrence, late of Wharf Street, Stoke-on-Trent, has removed to a commodius Pottery, which he has specially erected in Waterloo Street, Longton."

The company remained at the Falcon Works until 1957, when it joined its sister company Shaw & Copestake Ltd at their prestigious new pottery in Normacot Road, Longton. It ceased trading under its own name in 1962, and was finally wound up in 1964. The buildings of Falcon Works are now occupied by the John Beswick Company, (part of the Royal Doulton Group).

For many years Thomas Lawrence resided in Colwyn Bay, where he went on account of the health of his wife. But in spite of residing so far from the Potteries, Mr. Lawrence constantly maintained an active interest in the affairs of the Falcon Pottery until about twelve months prior to his death in April 1932.

On becoming a resident of Colwyn Bay Mr. Lawrence became involved with many local activities, including becoming manager of Bryn-y-Maen School. At his funeral, which took place at Bryn-y-Maen Church, the pupils of the school, one by one, laid bunches of daffodils on the grave. Mr. Lawrence was survived by his daughter, Mrs. F. Tucker and his sister Miss A. Lawrence.

JOHN GRUNDY, nephew of Thomas Lawrence joined his uncle at the Falcon Works in 1895. He became a partner in the company on 9th June 1920, although he had been solely responsible for the business for a number of years previous to this. The following is an extract from the Partnership Agreement:

'The said John Grundy shall at all times during the continuance of the partnership diligently employ himself in and about the business thereof and carry on and manage the same for its greatest benefit and advantage but the said Thomas Lawrence shall not be obliged to attend to the said business any further than he shall think proper'.

This indicates a desire by Thomas Lawrence to take a back seat, and he probably made the move to Colwyn Bay shortly after the partnership agreement. John Grundy married Florence Kathleen, they had one daughter Eileen, who married Mr. Richard Hull junior, managing director of Shaw & Copestake Ltd.

John Grundy was a talented artist, as can be seen by the signed painting on a vase dated 1897. This vase was found in a second hand shop by a collector, who recognised it from a photograph in The SylvaC Story. It was with another early vase on which Thomas Lawrence had experimented decorating a vase with a photograph of John Grundy. It was fortunate these vases were found as they were originally in The Manor House, the home of Mr. Grundy's daughter, where they had been photographed for The SylvaC Story. The house and contents were sold in 1995.

Mr. Grundy devoted himself almost solely to his business, and took no active part in public affairs, his chief concern was work. What little recreation he took was mostly devoted to angling, of which he was extremely fond. After Mr. Lawrence's death he became the owner of the business until he passed away on September 10th 1938 following a lengthy illness. This occurred three days after the firm became a limited company. Two accounts of his death appear in the Pottery Gazette, the first in September 1938 says he was in his 60th year, the second in October 1938 gives his age as 57.

Mr. Grundy became governing director and chairman of the new company, Thomas Lawrence (Longton) Ltd. After his untimely death the company was managed by Mr. Richard Hull who was Mr. Grundy's son-in-law, and Mr. Eric Dennis purchased Mr. Grundy's shares. The company continued to operate at the Falcon Works, until staff were moved to the new Sylvan Works, Normacot Road, Longton, and merged with Shaw & Copestake Ltd.

From 1942 to 1947 Thomas Lawrence (Longton) Ltd., shared their works with Shaw & Copestake Ltd., in order to comply with the Board of Trade Concentration of Industry Scheme. The Falcon Works was a more modern building than Shaw & Copestake's old pottery, and Mr. Richard Hull and his directors took the opportunity after the war to modernise the Shaw & Copestake works as far as was possible. The offices and showroom at the Falcon Works were much superior to those at Shaw & Copestake and Mr. Hull conducted the combined firms' business from a very plush private office at the Falcon Works. Mrs. May Alcock, company secretary, who had joined the company on leaving school, ran the day to day administrative affairs from an adjoining office.

Mr. REGINALD THOMPSON M.B.E. joined the company in 1917 at the age of 14. He started painting at the benches and extending lithos, and was awarded a scholarship to the Hanley School of Art, where he completed the course for pottery decorators and designers with distinction. He then applied for the position of decorating manager and Mr. John Grundy gave him a six months trial. In 1922 he became the youngest decorating manager in the Potteries at the age of 19.

He eventually became chief designer and modeller and retired in 1978 at the age of 75, having given the company over 60 years loyal service, he passed away in 1988 at the age of 85. His wife Gladys was a paintress at the Falcon Works, they had one daughter Jeanette, and were married for over 60 years. Mr. Thompson was awarded the British Empire Medal in recognition of his services to the pottery industry.

Mr. John Grundy, a partner in the company of Thomas Lawrence. He was with the firm from 1895 until his death in 1938.

Mr. Reginald Thompson at the Falcon Works c1923, he started as a painter and eventually became decorating manager and then chief designer.

Mr. Reginald Thompson flanked by fellow workers c1923.

wo views of the Falcon Works, Barford Street, ongton, taken in 1996. The property is now wned by The Royal Doulton Group.

Nº OF CERTIFICATE. 7

Nº OF SHARES. 750

THOMAS LAWRENCE (LONGTON), LIMITED.

INCORPORATED UNDER THE COMPANIES ACT, 1929.

CAPITAL £5000, divided into 5000 Shares of £1 each.

This is to Certify that Mrs Florence Kathleen Grundy *of* "Brackenlea", Weston Coyney, Stoke-on-Trent *is the Registered Proprietor of* Seven hundred and fifty *Fully Paid Shares of* One Pound *each numbered* 3,253 *to* 4,002 *both inclusive, in the above-named Company, subject to the Memorandum and Articles of Association of the said Company.*

Given under the Common Seal of the said Company, the Ninth *day of* February 1939

[signature] DIRECTORS.
[signature]

[signature] SECRETARY.

NO TRANSFER OF ANY OF THE ABOVE-MENTIONED SHARES CAN BE REGISTERED UNTIL THIS CERTIFICATE HAS BEEN DEPOSITED AT THE OFFICE OF THE COMPANY.

JORDAN & SONS, LIMITED, 116 TO 118, CHANCERY LANE, LONDON, W.C.2.

In 1938 the Thomas Lawrence company became limited. Shares were issued shortly afterwards, and this is a copy of the Share Certificate issued to Mrs. Florence Grundy, on the 9th February 1939.

THE PATENT OFFICE:
TRADE MARKS REGISTRY,

25, SOUTHAMPTON BUILDINGS,
LONDON, W.C.2. 24 NOV 1950

Thomas Lawrence (Longton) Limited

Gentlemen,

I have to inform you that the Registration of your Trade Mark No. 624660 in class 21 has been renewed for a period of 14 years from the 15th February 1951.

~~The renewal is advertised in No.~~
~~of the Trade Marks Journal.~~

I am, Gentlemen,
Your obedient Servant,
J. L. BLAKE,
Registrar.

The Falcon Ware trade mark had to be registered every fifteen years, this is a copy of the certificate issued in 1951.

CHAPTER TWO

VISIT TO MRS. EILEEN HULL AND AUCTION

Some years ago, about 1988, my husband Peter and I visited the daughter of Mr. John Grundy, Mrs. Eileen Hull widow of Mr. Richard Hull former managing director of Shaw & Copestake Ltd. Mrs. Hull resided at The Manor House, Leigh, Stoke-on-Trent, which was buried in the depths of the country. We had great difficulty in locating it, as none of the lanes had names, and there were no signposts. Much to our embarrassment we were at least half an hour late for our appointment when we drove up the impressive drive and through the wonderful wrought iron gates.

We were greeted at the door by a charming lady, whom we assumed was Mrs. Hull, and offered profuse apologies for our lateness. We were ushered into the lounge where another charming lady sat waiting for us, so we offered the same profuse apologies, and wondered if this was the lady of the house. We addressed our conversation to both, trying to weigh up in our minds which was Mrs. Hull, and this state of affairs continued until the conversation gradually led to the clarification of the situation. (It was Mrs. Hull who had greeted us at the door and her companion who sat in the lounge).

Great relief on our part, as we could now direct the correct questions to the right lady! Mrs. Hull was already over 80 years old, but very active and articulate and pleased to help with our researches. Although there were no catalogues or documents of the company which was a disappointment, there were plenty of examples of the products, and we were taken to almost every room in the Manor House and shown a variety of Falcon Ware and SylvaC. Mrs. Hull also told us of her involvement with the new products and how Mr. Hull often brought the latest designs home for her opinion. She told us how she had run the works canteen during the war, how her father John Grundy had known the name of every person working at the factory, and that he paid 1d a week health insurance for each employee. She showed us the paintings her father had done, and a vase he had painted with a lion dated 1897. Unfortunately many of the ornaments had damage to them, and were glued together.

We saw many unusual pieces which I photographed and made notes about, and Mrs. Hull was particularly kind to us, escorting us from the basement to attic in the search of Falcon Ware. We also recorded the interview which was very useful, as it is always difficult to remember exact conversations. We were shown family photographs, and for the first time we saw the Falcon figures of Jeanette, the Water Carrier and the little girl sitting. It was a beautiful house, tastefully furnished, full of Falcon Ware and SylvaC history and an experience we will never forget.

AUCTION

Unfortunately Mrs. Hull became seriously ill and is now looked after in a nursing home. It was decided by those responsible for her financial affairs, and as there was no immediate family, to auction the house and its contents.

An initial sale of general house contents took place on Tuesday 9th May 1995 at the Louis Taylor Auction Rooms, 10 Town Street, Hanley. We were unable to attend the auction, but managed to view the Lots on Friday 5th May. We knew immediately we were in the right place as our attention was drawn to two vases with familiar decorations, SHEILA and GRECIAN. This was a very sad occasion as there in the auction room wer many of the ornaments and vases we had seen on our visit, bu looking rather forlorn.

Our first concern was not to purchase the Falcon Ware c SylvaC, but to search for catalogues and paperwork. We foun a suitcase which contained some interesting photographs, sever other separate Lots of framed photographs, and boxes full c books, but much to our disappointment no catalogues. Howeve we left bids for the Lots which we thought of particular interes mainly photographs and books.

We were successful in only one bid, which was a set of fou miniatures, hand coloured photographs of the Hull family, I wa very happy with these but disappointed about the other los items. My main fear was that the family photographs would b discarded, as they probably held no interest for the purchaser

My first bit of luck occurred almost immediately. I ha reported back to Mick Collins of the SylvaC Collectors Circl who had been unable to attend the auction, telling him of th Lots I had missed. Shortly after, he telephoned to say one c the Lots, a suitcase and box containing photographs and book was in his possession, it had been purchased by an acquaintanc who, realising its importance had bought it for him. Good new indeed, as I was to be allowed to borrow these for my researc

I then wrote to the two other purchasers of Lots I wa interested in, via the auctioneer, Louis Taylor, who kindly passe the letters on. One of the photographs I was anxious to obtai was of John Grundy, and the lady and gentleman who bough this sent it to me immediately with their compliments. Eventuall the other purchasers telephoned me, offering the family photo graphs, they were quite happy to part with them (they ha bought them for the frames). So after several weeks all the Hu family photographs eventually joined the rest of the Thoma Lawrence archives, which I have painstakingly gathere together. We have always thought the people of Staffordshir exceedingly friendly, helpful and kind, and this episod reinforced our views.

A final footnote to this tale involves two early Falcon War vases photographs of which appeared in The SylvaC Story. On was a vase with a lion handpainted by John Grundy dated 189 the other had a photograph of John Grundy superimposed on th vase, a method Thomas Lawrence had been experimenting wit It was one of the photographs we had taken on our visit to Mr Hull and although the vases were damaged, as many of th ornaments were, they were two of the earliest Falcon War pieces I had seen.

As these were not in the auction I was rather concerned abou their fate and wondered what had happened to them. Howeve they were discovered by vigilant and enthusiastic collectors, i a bric-a-brac shop in Stoke-on-Trent, who remembered seein the photograph in the book. They were bought for a bargai price and are an important part of Falcon Ware history. S although much of the Hull family home has been dispersed a least many items are now cherished by Falcon Ware collectors

The rest of the finer house contents were disposed of at later auction of Fine Arts, which took place on the 6th June The Manor House, land, stable block and paddock was sold a auction in four lots, by order of the Court of Protection, at th Crown Hotel, Stone, Staffordshire on September 27th 1995.

◀ Mrs. Eileen Hull, daughter of Mr. John Grundy shows me a Falcon Ware ginger jar, on our visit to her home c1988. The house contents were auctioned during May and June 1995, photographs of some of the auction items appear on the following pages.

▼ The Manor House, home of Mrs. Eileen Hull, was sold at auction on 27th September 1995. It had contained some unusual pieces of Falcon Ware and SylvaC.

All these photographs and on the opposite page were taken at the viewing of the Lots prior to the auction.

◄ The Breton Girl.

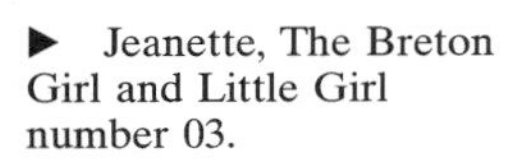

► Jeanette, The Breton Girl and Little Girl number 03.

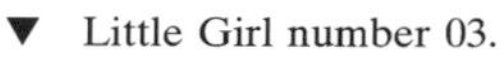

▼ Little Girl number 03.

▼ Two polar bears, and two cats number 3151.

▲ Falcon Ware teapot with blue and pink flowers.

▲ Two red and white spotted toadstools.

SylvaC cat number 1313 and SylvaC carthorse number 4963.

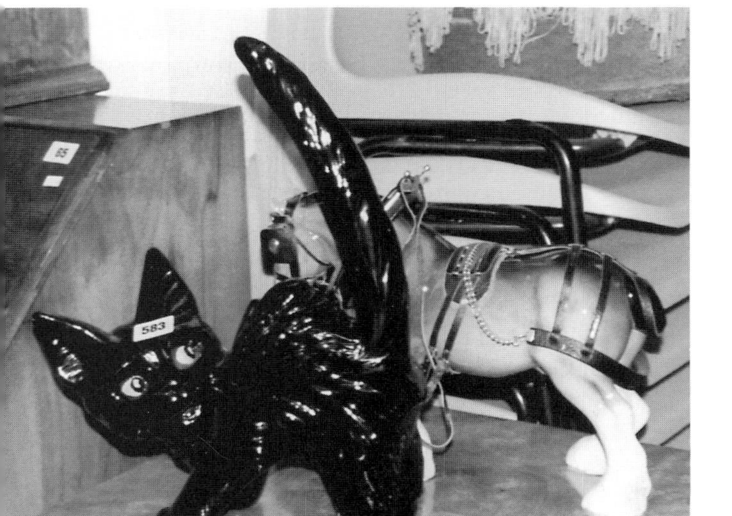

▼ Mr. Pickwick type character ornament.

▼ SylvaC animals and posy and Falcon Ware Indian head bookends.

CHAPTER THREE

PRODUCTS OF THE FACTORY

Products of the Thomas Lawrence, Falcon Works were considered middle of the range, stylish and tasteful. There was no question of any ugly shapes or designs. There were many potteries in competition for the same markets, but the innovative decorations of Thomas Lawrence still stand out amongst other wares. Judging by the number of pieces found in Australia there was also a thriving export market.

VASES, FLOWER JUGS AND ROSE BOWLS

Many vases made by the Thomas Lawrence factory were unmarked, making identification difficult. Recognition of impressed or raised shape names and numbers on the base of wares is of great importance. Two digit numbers were in use in the late 1890's and in the early 1900's, by 1924 number 120 was in use, reaching 253 in the 1940's. In the 1940's the shape or mould numbers started again at number one reaching 759 when the company merged with Shaw & Copestake in 1957. But some of the old numbers were absorbed into the new numbers if they were popular designs. The shape names very often covered a range of wares with the same basic shape in different sizes.

Attractive embossed patterns were produced, with heron, kingfisher, and flower designs, and even an owl shaped vase. There is also a delightful flower jug with a butterfly handle, one with a kingfisher handle and a range of Deco style vases and flower jugs. Many of the flower jugs and vases continued to be produced by Shaw & Copestake after World War II, and often bore the SylvaC mark, one of the most popular being the ALEX jug which can be found in a variety of decorations.

The MASONA rose bowl is the one most often found in collections, and can be found in many different stunning patterns. The CASKET rose bowl was produced in a plain shape as well as embossed with a kingfisher which is particularly attractive and can be a basic blue or brown hue, fortunately this piece has a Registered Design Number 794854 which dates it at 1934 (the only piece I have seen with this type of number). Other rose bowls are called FALCON, WINDSOR, ACME, MARSH and CROMER. Plant pots were given the names CLIFTON (also a vase), TOKIO and BRON, the ART pots were produced in three sizes. Only recently Marie Hammond in Australia sent photographs of two plant pots impressed with the name LOUIS (large size) and LOUIS 2 (small size), one of which has a gold circle surrounding 'Made in England'. They are decorated with the same pattern as found on her ART pots (which are marked Falcon Ware), and have a scalloped rim and ornamental handles. Marie also found a vase impressed LONDON with the same decoration. It is more than likely these are Thomas Lawrence Falcon Ware. After World War II, and in the SylvaC years many more vases, flower jugs and plant pots were designed and produced at the Falcon Works, and these are well documented in the books The SylvaC Story and The SylvaC Companion.

TABLEWARE

Butter dishes, one called FLORAL shape which has a flower handle, and cheese dishes BRISTOL and EMPIRE were amongst the shapes produced, but many others had no known shape names to identify them by. Sometimes the Falcon Wa mark and decoration name or number is in the lid of the dis Several designs of teapots i.e. DUTCH, PARIS and CHESTE and coffee pots, honey pots and biscuit barrels were manufa tured. The DUTCH shape was also used for jug sets, and h water jugs, and the PARIS shape included a coffee pot ar ewer. Cake plates and stands, sandwich sets, salad and fruit se handled bowls and bread plates were also produced. I have on seen one shape of bread plate, but with many different pattern

The general purpose Falcon Ware jugs are often seen at Antiq Fairs, and came in various styles, decorations and sizes, BRISTO CUBAN, DUTCH, OBAN, are the impressed names, but oth shapes have no known names. They were usually bought ori inally in sets of three but I have recently seen for the first tim a very small DUTCH shape cream jug, only 2⅜" high.

I have a little sales notebook which belonged to H.F. Wo dated 1932 in which the wholesale prices of wares is writte and I found this fascinating. For example six doz jugs in 'slig Cornish' design were three shillings, and four toilet sets in Cam and Palm design were one shilling. Twelve 210 vases were si pence, considering all the processes one vase went throug including the decorating, it seems incredibly cheap.

The nursery tableware was decorated with bears, and mic and later on included koala bears with a kangaroo edging. Som of the decorations have the names Jeanette Ruth in one corne and these are the names of Reginald Thompson's daught (Jeanette) and Eric Dennis's daughter Ruth. Of the tw examples seen with the names, one is still in the possession Jeanette, and the other is with an Australian collector.

In 1938 Mr. Reginald Thompson designed the Wishing We range of tableware, comprising an attractive hand painte embossed flower and stone effect, which continued to be pr duced until the 1950's. There was a limited range of tablewa with embossed flowers, called Springtime, but this is rarely se and comprised leaf shaped dishes, honey pot, salad bowls, ar various sized plates and dishes. During the SylvaC years oth tableware was designed by Mr. Thompson, amongst them Dov cote range and Hydrangea range.

TOILET WARE AND TRINKET SETS

Toilet sets seem to have been the Thomas Lawrence specialit as there are many different styles, some ornate and others pla but all beautifully decorated. They all appear to have sha range names, and are constantly referred to in the Pattern Bo and other documents such as sales lists and shipping orders. T shape range names cover all the items in a toilet set and al some of the trinket sets. One of the earliest was ELITE referr to in the early 1900's, also popular were FALCON, RETO EMPIRE, CORINTH, CHATSWORTH, CITY, HADDON ar BUNGALOW, (others are shown in the register of shape nam page 151). The chamber pots were referred to in the stock lis of 1949, but the toilet sets had probably ceased production then.

The trinket sets came in two sizes, 7 piece or 10 piece. T trays have been found in two shapes, but the accessories vary design. Sometimes the trinket boxes have an impressed sha

(continued page 12

◀ ▶ These photographs were taken at the home of Mrs. Eileen Hull before the contents were auctioned. The vases were subsequently found in a second hand shop in Stoke-on-Trent, and rescued by a dilligent collector. They are very damaged, the one on the left is an early attempt by Mr. Thomas Lawrence to decorate pottery by photography, the photograph is of Mr. John Grundy. The vase on the right is hand painted by Mr. John Grundy, signed and dated 1897.

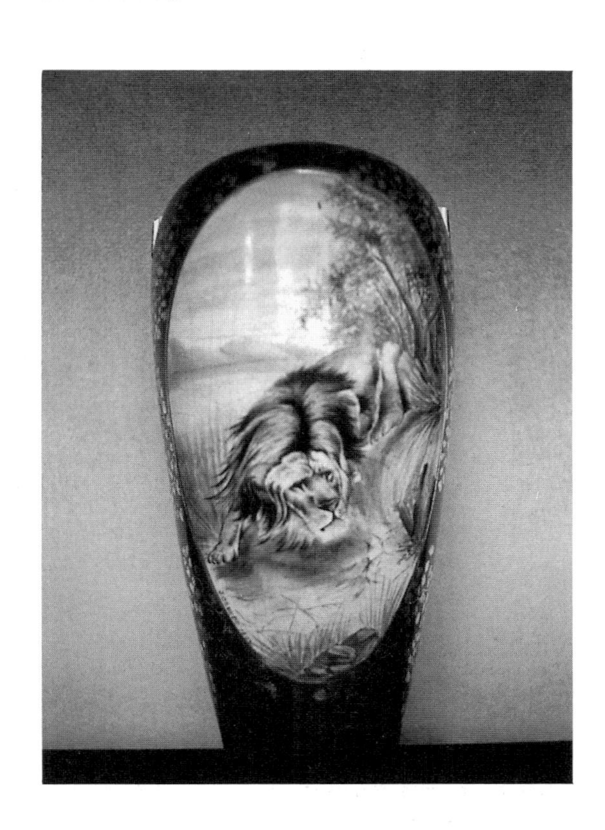

▼ Vase impressed with the name LONDON 11″ high. It has no Thomas Lawrence mark, but the decoration has been seen on other products.

▼ Plant pot impressed with the name LOUIS 8″ high. It has a gold circle around Made in England on the base. Both photographs from Marie Hammond.

▲ Left, vases impressed 120, decoration number 4153, gold circle around Made in England, and the words English Make. Right, impressed HADDON 11″ high, decoration number 4153. They both have a black ground. Photograph from Janice and Terry Waller.

▲ Shape number 184 14″ high, decoration number 4437, Falcon Glendoza Ware, (in a column) is printed within a laurel wreath. The pattern is embossed on a black ground. Photograph from Pauline Thake.

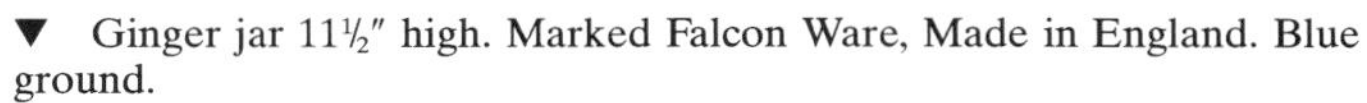

▼ Ginger jar 11½″ high. Marked Falcon Ware, Made in England. Blue ground.

▼ Shape HADDON 11″ high, decoration number 4173H. Photograph from Janice and Terry Waller.

▲ English ALTON Make, (in a column) is impressed on the base of the vases, they are 17½″ high. The ginger jar is 14″ high. Decoration number 4153. Photograph from Shona McNeill.

▲ Shape is TOKIO, decoration 4153, 8″ high. From Denise and Paul Tripp.

▼ Shape is GLOBE No. 1, decoration 4153, 11″ high 12″ wide. Photograph from Janice and Terry Waller.

▲ ALGIERS vase 10″ high, CLIFTON pot 7½″ high, 215 vases 15″ high, all with ZEELAND decoration. Photograph from Janice and Terry Waller.

▼ HADDON No. 2 vases 9¼″ high, decoration number 4624, pink poppies on black ground. Photograph from Sheila Cox.

▼ WINDSOR rose bowl, decoration number 4624, 6½″ high 11″ wide. Photograph from Helen Jamieson.

"FALCON" WARE SHAPES

LOCK
REGAL No. 1
MODERN
SYDNEY
EMPRESS
CRESCENT

218
SIAM
22
HOLLON No. 2
215
OREON
223
ALADDIN
217

ALEX No. 1
206
DAINTY
RYDER
ARRON
220
ALEX No. 2

CLIFTON No. 2
SUDAN POT
ALGIERS
WESTERN
SUDAN
BOUQUET

THOS. LAWRENCE (LONGTON) LTD., FALCON WORKS, LONGTON, STOKE-ON-TRENT.

Vase number 22 is misprinted and should be 226.

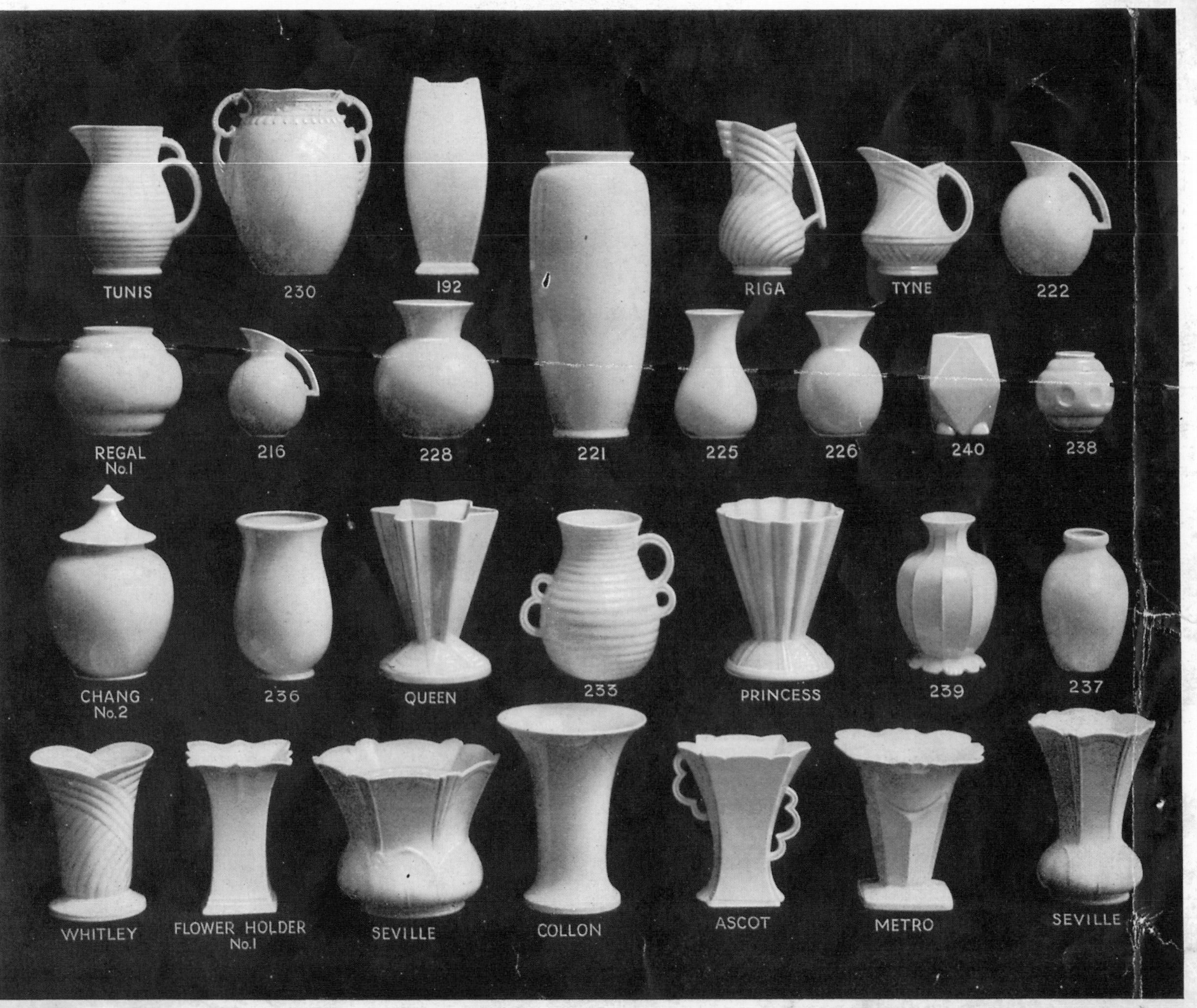

'FALCON" WARE SHAPES
TUNIS
230
192
RIGA
TYNE
222
REGAL No.1
216
228
221
225
226
240
238
CHANG No.2
236
QUEEN
233
PRINCESS
239
237
WHITLEY
FLOWER HOLDER No.1
SEVILLE
COLLON
ASCOT
METRO
SEVILLE
THOS. LAWRENCE (LONGTON) LTD. FALCON WORKS, LONGTON, STOKE ON TRENT

◀ ELITE shape toilet set, decoration number 4850. Photograph from Marie Hammond.

▶ Tray from a trinket set. It has no shape name or decoration number, but 'A bit of old England' is on the front of the decoration. It has an attractive border of thatched cottages.

These small vases are found with toilet or trinket ts. Shape names from the left, BUNGALOW, HATSWORTH, RETON and VICTOR. The heights e 4½″, 5½″, 5½″, 4½″, they have no decoration numbers, ıt VICTOR vase has 'The Old Mill' written on the ont. They were all popular Falcon Ware decorations.

▲ TOWER shape toilet set, decoration number 4281, with yellow ground. Photograph from John Stiles.

▲ Jug 5″ high, decoration number 5109, 'Alton' on the front. Photograph from Jean Simms.

▲ OBAN jug, (one of a set of three, 5″ high, 6″ high, 6½″ high), decoration number 4911. Photograph from Jean Simms.

▲ This Falcon Ware chamber pot has no decoration number. Photograph from Jackie and Tony Chew.

◄ BUNGALOW shape toilet set, with the popular Camel and Palm decoration Photograph from Grace Fin

◀ CHATSWORTH shape toilet and trinket set. Decoration number 4548. Photograph from John Paley.

▼ Chamber pot with unusual ribbed effect. Photograph by Jackie and Tony Chew.

VICTOR shape toilet set, decoration umber 5141, called 'Lady and Dovecote'. hotograph from Brian Stalley.

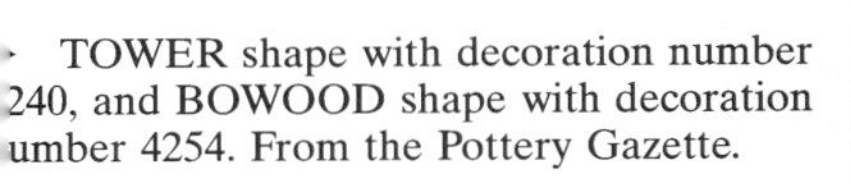

TOWER shape with decoration number 240, and BOWOOD shape with decoration umber 4254. From the Pottery Gazette.

◀ FALCON shape toilet jug approximately 11″ high, the matching bowl is the same as BUNGALOW shape. The decoration number is 4965. Photograph from Jean Simms.

▼ Falcon Ware jugs, and with the 'Argosy' Galleon decoration the DUTCH jugs and teapots. Photograph lent by Mick and Derry Collins.

◀ DUTCH hot water jug 6″ high, PARIS coffee pot 7″ high, decoration number 4745g, (Dolly Varden).

▶ PARIS teapot, decoration number 5126, (S & C Cottage Scene). Photograph from Brian Stalley.

▼ DUTCH teapot, pattern number 4745, (Dolly Varden). From Brian Stalley.

▼ No. 2 DUTCH B jug, bluetits on apple blossom 5″ high. From the late Mr. Reginald Thompson's collection.

name on the base, these are usually the same names as the toilet sets as the range covered quite a large number of wares. Children's miniature trinket sets were also produced, but I have yet to see any of these items.

ANIMALS

A small pre-war range of animals was produced and these consisted of two dogs one called BINKY and a spaniel called LADY. Polar bears appeared to be popular and as well as the free standing version, there was a choice of one or two bears standing or climbing on ice or rocks. There was also a very splendid two bear table lamp beautifully modelled by Mr. Reg Thompson, a real masterpiece. Other wild animals included a small leopard lying close to the ground, and there also appears to be a small elephant with a downward trunk, similar to the later number 92 which proved to be very popular.

There is a wonderful seagull on a rock, and Jeanette, Reg Thompson's daughter found the original drawing of this amongst his books. This was one of the pieces we saw at Mrs. Eileen Hull's home, it was eventually auctioned. A falcon wall plaque can be seen in an old photograph (see page 124), in the same photograph can be seen a pelican or duck with open beak and one or two other animals which are difficult to identify.

Just before the Second World War, a special order of large pigs, about 14″ long, were made for a butcher's shop. These were never collected, perhaps due to the onset of war, and were stored in the warehouse for many years. They were eventually sold c1947, and a special photograph was taken for The Bulletin (the staff magazine), in which five pigs can be seen, to celebrate the event. (This photograph is reproduced in The SylvaC Companion page 136).

There are also two other pigs, a sow three and a half inches long, and piglet one and a half inches long.

NOVELTIES

Some very interesting pre-war novelties emerged from the Falcon Works, there is a colourful series of red and white spotted toadstools, one of which is a candle holder, but the others appear to be purely ornamental. A frog on an ashtray has been found by a collector, it has not been possible to date this as it has no number on the base, and it may be post war.

Three types of pre-war book-ends are known, the Indian head book-ends are very colourfully decorated, and I have a copy of the original drawing by Reg Thompson. This is quite well documented, it is also mentioned in the Pattern Book, number 4961, c1935 along with a sketch. The preceding numbers, 4959 and 4960, are cock book-ends, also sketched, but I have yet to see these in real life. A pair of squirrel book-ends found by a collector, both quite clearly marked, are not mentioned in any paper work. This is a good example of the importance of collectors reporting their purchases thus enabling us to record the details.

The TOUCAN with MELBOURNE bowl, comes in three sizes of TOUCAN and two sizes of MELBOURNE bowl, all stunningly decorated. I had a phone call from a gentleman who inherited a TOUCAN and bowl in GRECIAN pattern from his grandmother. He is certain this was bought in 1915 for twopence, and although the TOUCAN is not mentioned in the pattern book until 1932, it is possible it was in production before that date. However, it would be wise to keep an open mind about the dates until further confirmation. The TOUCAN is possibly the best known piece of early Falcon Ware, and I know of one collector who has at least six sets in his collection, all with different decorations.

The PARROT with SYDNEY bowl is not quite so well known, very few seem to be in existence, it was still in production in 1939. I have the PARROT in my collection but it was broug over from Australia for me by a visiting collector. I know only one other in this country, and one in Australia. Bo TOUCAN and PARROT are flower holders, and according have appertures in the base to accommodate flowers. The bow are usually referred to as float bowls, originally intended f floating flowers in.

FIGURES

Jeanette and Joan, flower girls are probably the best know Thomas Lawrence figures, and are typical 1930's girls, very fem nine and delicately decorated in pastel colours. They are iden ical in features and styles, but vary in height, Jeanette is 10½ high and Joan is 8½″ high. The names are usually stamped gold on the base.

Other figures include the Breton Girl, the Water Carri Mary, Pierrette, Priscilla, and Orange Seller. These are all pr war, although some may have continued in production until t 1950's. They are all illustrated in this book, the colourings the figures can vary, but they are usually handpainted in natur colours. The exception being Pierrette found in green ma Some years ago a dealer had a green Pierrette for sale whi had Made in England on the base, but no other markings. The was much debate as to whether this was SylvaC or not, and thought not as the style of base was quite different to the usu SylvaC figures. Just for interest I photographed it on the st hoping I would be able to identify it one day. Having studi the photograph taken of the Thomas Lawrence stand at t British Industries Fair, I am sure there is a Pierrette on the thi shelf down centre left of the picture, which seems very like t photograph I took on the dealers stand. (See page 122)

The figure of a little girl sitting on a chair nursing a doll does n appear to have a name. She is 6½″ high, and I first saw her at t home of Mrs. Eileen Hull, she then appeared for sale at the auctio The only other known example is in the collection of Mick a Derry Collins, but I have no doubt others will surface befo long. On the base the number 03 is impressed, one of the fir products of the new numbering system started c1940.

I was most envious when a collector sent me a photograph a cherubic looking choir boy, and was delighted when I fou the same figure some months later. He is 6″ high, superb modelled and decorated and has the number 09 impressed the base, indicating he is an early 1940's product.

The avuncular figure entitled Mine Host, is an inn keep standing beside a barrel and two jugs. Although the only tw examples I have seen were in the possession of Mrs. Eileen Hu (daughter of John Grundy), and were sold to a collector the auction of her house contents, it is possible others we produced.

Three Dickensian type characters in the form of spill holde Mr. Pickwick, The Farmer's Boy and The Farmer's Wife, we also produced by Thomas Lawrence. The last two characte also appear on jugs, tankards and wall plaques. There were al several character jugs, John Bull was a pre-war model, Di Turpin, Henry VIII, Punch and Cavalier all originated at t Falcon Pottery, were given new numbers and included in t Shaw & Copestake range. The Cavalier jugs and wall plaqu were originally a Falcon Ware pre-war design, this was extend after the war, and a completely new range launched in 1976 Shaw & Copestake.

Many animals, birds, novelties or fancies were produced the Thomas Lawrence Falcon Works after the war, continui until they merged with Shaw & Copestake in 1957. As a resu many of the original Falcon Ware designs have a SylvaC mar some continued to be produced until Shaw & Copestake w taken over by Longton Ceramics in 1982. Even then, Longt Ceramics and later Crown Winsor still used some of the Falc

(continued page 12

Stunning polar bear table lamp lent by Jeanette Holdcroft.

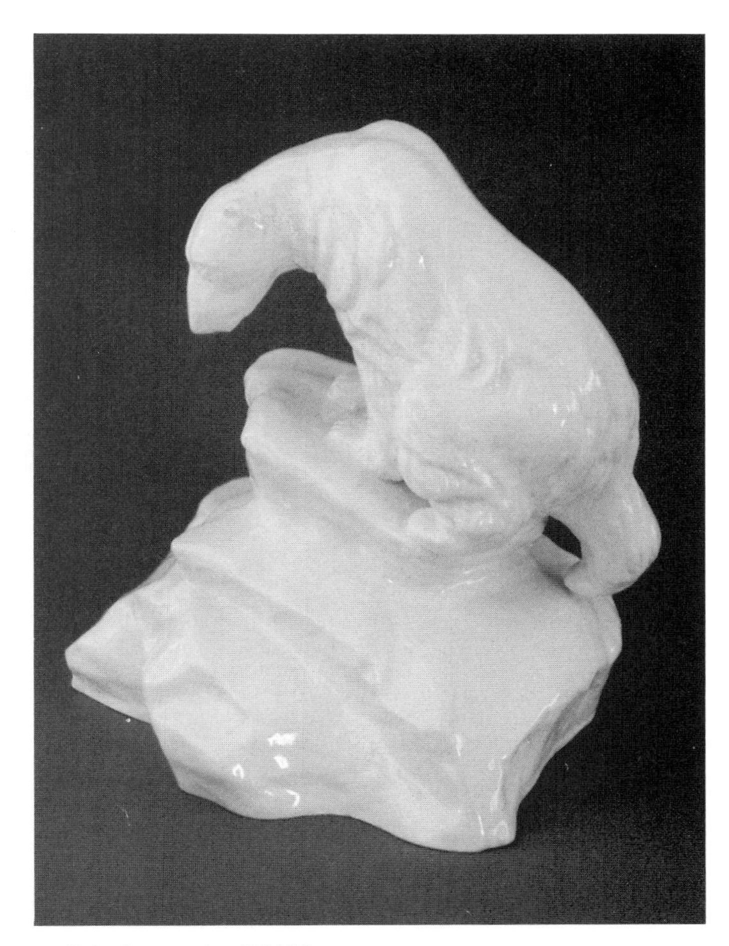

▲ Polar bear on ice 6½″ high.

◄ Polar bear on ice 7″ high. Photograph from Jackie and Tony Chew. All the animals on this page were designed and modelled by Reginald Thompson.

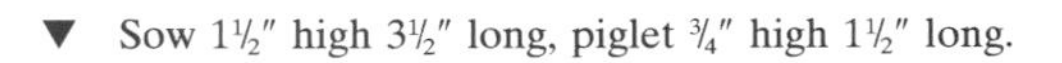

▼ Sow 1½″ high 3½″ long, piglet ¾″ high 1½″ long.

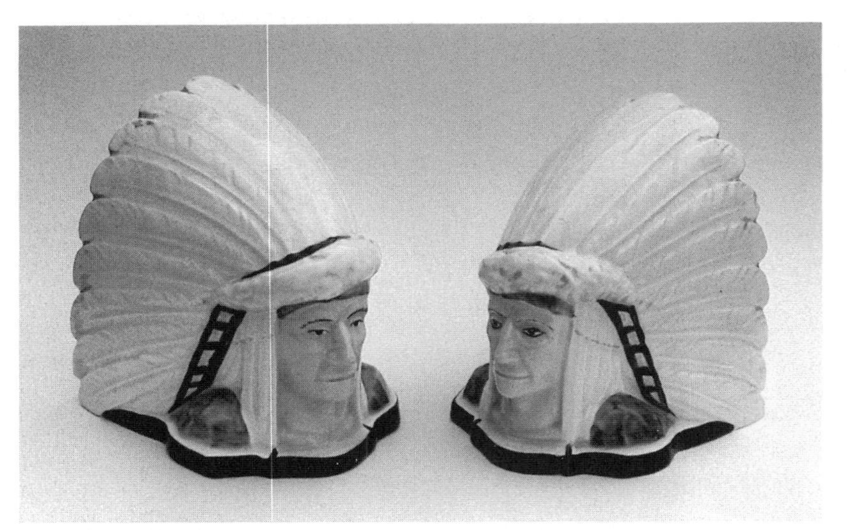

▲ Indian head bookends 5″ high, decoration number 4961.

►▲ Green matt pierrette seen on Sheila and Jim Piper's stall at Alexandra Palace some years ago. Possibly Falcon Ware, see photograph on page 124.

◄ Superb model of 'Mine Host'.

▼ These form only part of the Toucan collection of Janice and Terry Waller. Here are four large 9½″ high, one small beak down 6″ high, and one small beak up 7½″ high. The decorations are GRECIAN, FANTASTIC and KILLARNEY. Photograph from Janice and Terry Waller.

Pickwickian type ornament 4¼″ high.

▲ Priscilla 7″ high, this was slightly remodelled at a later date.

Angelic choirboy 6½″ high.

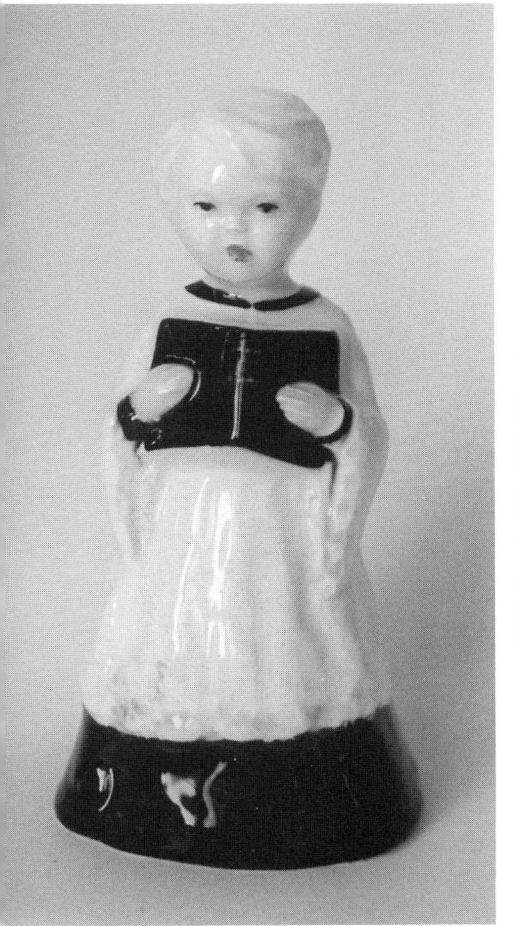

▼ The Farmer's wife 4¾″ high and The Farmer's Boy 4½″ high, have a small container at the back for spills.

Photograph of the Thomas Lawrence (Longton) Ltd. stand, taken at the British Industries Fair in 1939. Kindly lent by Mick and Derry Collins.

nd SylvaC moulds that were included with the purchase of the orks.

It is known that Reginald Thompson designed or modelled e majority of the animals, novelties and figures. His daughter eanette Holdcroft allowed us access to his papers, amongst hich we found many of his original drawings and sketches, or rints which gave him an idea for a model. The number of nimals modelled gradually increased after the war, when his lent was recognised by the management of Shaw & Copestake.

CLOCK SETS

here are four known types of clock sets, two have the impressed ame on the bases of the clock and vases, ESSEX and CLAY-ON. Two other styles have also been found, but no shape ames are on the base. In the Pattern Book, the LONDON ock set is mentioned, and a collector has seen a clock impressed THENS (but unmarked), these have yet to be identified, though only recently a vase with the impressed name ONDON, has been found. They were decorated in a variety typical Falcon Ware patterns, and were probably first pro-uced late 1920's-early 1930's. They are small simply styled ocks, not at all grotesque or ornate as so many of the china ocks were. I believe production of the clocks discontinued after 940.

COMMEMORATIVE WARE

A small amount of commemorative ware was produced by Thomas Lawrence, and very few items have been found to date. A DUTCH jug commemorating the coronation of HRH King George VI, 12th May 1937 is safely in the hands of collector Brian Stalley, who refuses to part with it. On a trip to Guernsey I found two beautiful jugs commemorating the same 1937 coronation. I gave these to our daughter, and she has kindly let me borrow them again for a photograph! Consequently I still have to add a piece of commemorative ware to my own collection. Incidentally there were quite a few nice pieces of Falcon Ware in Guernsey, but I managed to resist the temptation to struggle over to the mainland with them.

A recent find by collector Jackie proved to be of considerable interest as it commemorates an event that occurred in Trentham Gardens, Trentham, Stoke-on-Trent. It is a mug of 3½" high, has 'Trentham August 1940' on the back, and on the front a shield surrounded by an entwined blue ribbon on which is inscribed 'FIRST OUTCASTS ANNIVERSARY. AUGUST 1939 – AUGUST 1940'. This wartime event has inspired two local newspaper articles, both of which are reproduced by kind permission of The Sentinal Newspapers. One dated November 1992 actually shows photographs of the mug, which was manufactured as a momento of the first anniversary of the arrival of 1,000 banking staff and other workers from London. Jackie was lucky enough to purchase this important piece of Staffordshire history for only £10.00 and as I have kept the newspaper cutting since 1992 you can imagine how thrilled I was to receive her letter requesting information about the piece.

No. 2 DUTCH B jug 5¼" high. The Coronation of His Majesty ing George VI and Her Majesty Queen Elizabeth, 12th May 1937. ent by Brian Stalley.

◄ Two Coronation jugs 5¾" high and 7¼" high. Lent by Jayne and David Richards.

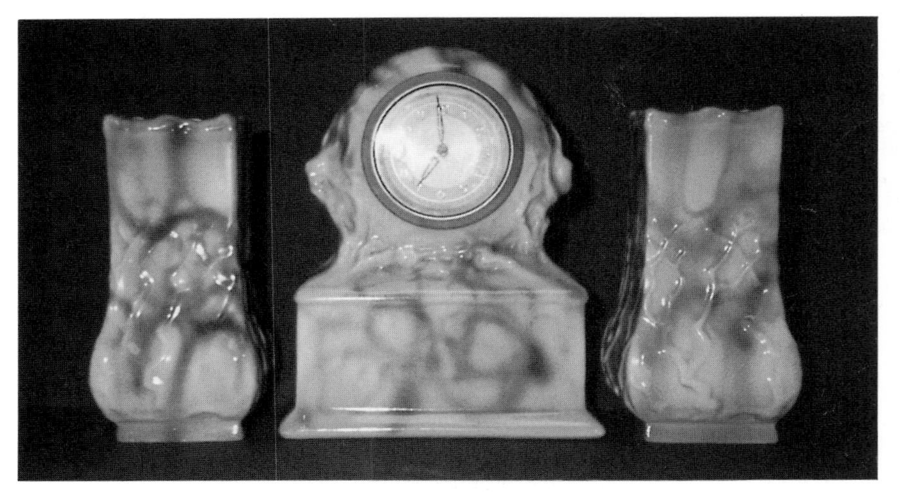

◀ CLAYTON clock 6¼″ high, vases 5″ high, GRECIAN decoration. Photograph from Malcolm Harris.

▶ ESSEX clock set, dated 1931. Photograph from Malcolm Harris.

▼ Clock 11½″ high 9″ wide. Photograph from Jane R. Hallsworth.

▲ Clock 8¼″ high, vases 7″ high, decoration number 4453. Photograph from Jane R. Hallsworth.

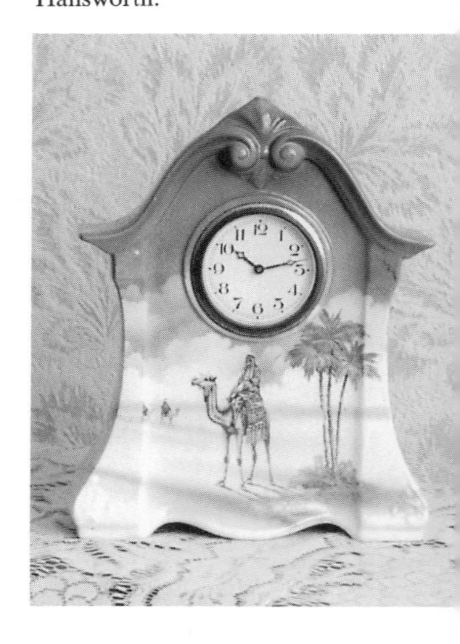

Wartime secret spot recalled

ONLY people of the wartime generation are likely to know hat the ballroom building t Trentham Gardens once oused the Bank of ngland, or at least a part of .

I have been reminded of the time hen Trentham was a top-secret deaway by a picture of a comme- orative mug made in August 1940 mark the first anniversary of the rival of more than 1,000 banking aff and other workers from London.

These exiles from the metropolis ve themselves the collective nick- ame of "The Outcasts" and used it the title of a magazine and for any groups and teams. The name is inted on the mug, owned by a afford family.

The handsome memento was made Falcon Ware, T Lawrence Ltd, d there can't be many about now. ow many other people, I wonder, ill have one? And where was Falcon 'are?

Graham Bebbington, local author d historian, tells me that Trentham ardens was the central clearing use for the banks, including a ction of the Bank of England, and so accommodated staff of the Pay- aster-General and the Inland evenue.

Apparently, the move to Trentham as completed over one weekend st before war was declared in 1939. e staff travelled in two special ains and the equipment was trans- rted by road.

"The operation had been planned r months," says Graham, "and on e Monday morning they were ready r business."

The clearing bank had its own post fice and every night a huge con- gnment of mail was taken across the ad to the old Trentham Gardens ilway station.

● Two sides of the commemorative mug produced for Bank of England and other staff based at Trentham Gardens during the war. Picture by T Symons, Stafford. *(See "Wartime secret spot . . .").*

"The Outcasts" lodged at homes all over the area and stayed until 1946. Some married local people and never returned to London at all. One of these was Lady Nancy Bryan, who met her husband Sir Arthur Bryan while both were working at Trentham.

▲ This interesting article was sent to me by Malcolm Harris in November 1992, and is reproduced with the permission of The Evening Sentinel, of The Staffordshire Sentinel Newspapers Ltd.

Jackie Kaldenburg has actually found one of the unique commemorative ugs, it is 3½″ high, and in perfect condition.

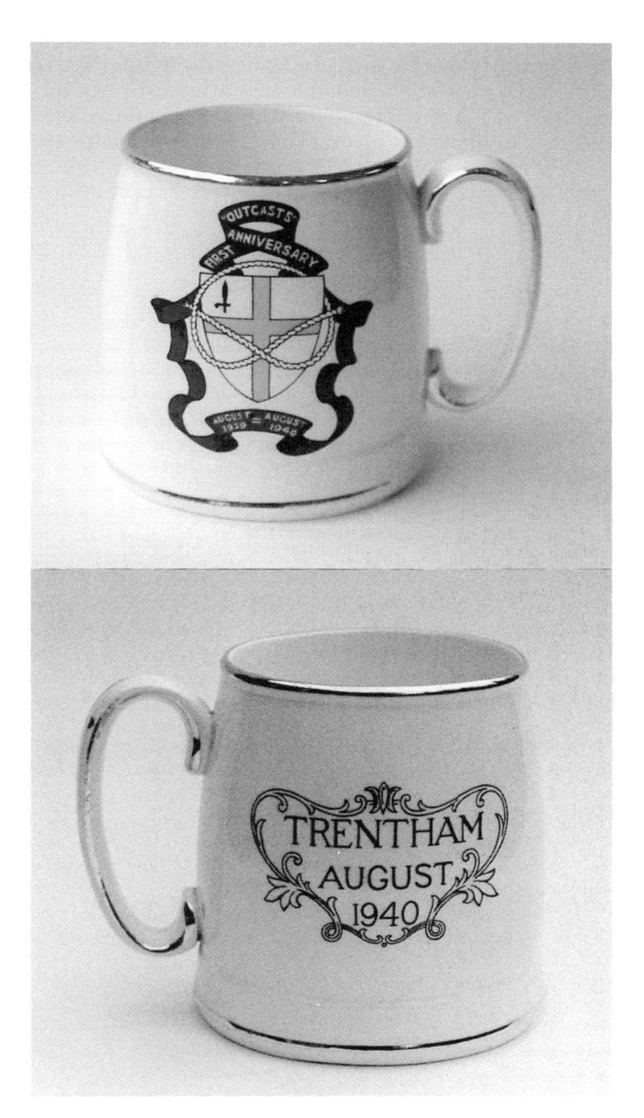

CHAPTER FOUR

TYPES OF DECORATIONS USED ON THOMAS LAWRENCE WARES

It is generally accepted that most potteries adopt their own type of decorating, creating unique 'in house' styles and designs in the hope of catching the eye of the buyers. Due to the number of lithographs used it is inevitably difficult to achieve this. Sometimes lithographs used are of similar themes to other potteries, with subtle differences and extensions, the Japanese Lady, Crinoline Lady, Camel and Palm and Swallows in Flight, come to mind as prime examples. These were popular designs and although it was important to create a 'style' which became associated with the manufacturer, it was tempting to jump on the bandwagon of the latest trend. In the late 1930's and early 1940's it is accepted that Shaw & Copestake and Thomas Lawrence interchanged lithos and designs and this continued when they worked from the same factory during the war years.

In the early 1900's, roses were the most popular decoration outnumbering all other flowers. By 1910 decorative bands and Chintz patterns were also used, and during the First World War although roses still predominated, Chinese Willow, Oriental Birds, and Oriental Poppy patterns were introduced. In the 1920's more use was made of the decorative bands with a solid ground colour, and black became fashionable, decorated and lined or stippled with gold paste. Other patterns of this era were fairly typical such as fruit, swallows, kingfishers, boats, waterlilies, Chinese lanterns, Geisha, camel and palm, and the old English scenes.

During the 1930's amongst other new patterns were the Cornish scene, Dutch figures, 'Good Old Times', 'Bit of Old England' 'Old Manor Garden' and Dolly Varden described as a 'Victorian Garden Scene', (this is the lady in the yellow crinoline). From The Concise Oxford Dictionary '***Dolly Varden: Kinds of woman's hat and dress. (Character in Barnaby Rudge)***.' Blue and white clouds were used as an extension of lithos, blue edging and multi-coloured bands were still relied upon and feature on many of Thomas Lawrence wares.

It is interesting to note Thomas Lawrence never used the cellulose finish so popular with Shaw & Copestake, but continued with the traditional method of glazing. Some of the wares have a black satin ground, or a bright blue ground which gives the decorations tremendous impact. Matt glaze ware was produced during the Second World War, mainly on SylvaC shapes.

The method of decoration associated with and unique to Thomas Lawrence are the multi-coloured abstract aerographed designs. By far the most popular design was called GRECIAN ovals in shades of orange and touches of green and brow this was a freehand style resulting in every piece being slightl different. KADIS is similar with the additional colours of blu and purple, there are many patterns in the range, GEORGI ASSYRIAN, FLAMAR, CHINESE, KILLARNEY, ITALIA BURMA. One collector has dated the GRECIAN pattern early as 1915, and as this can be neither proved or disproved the moment it would be advisable to keep an open mind about i Others, have associated these designs with Reginald Thompson Aerographing Department, and I had always thought of the as very typically his style, however he didn't become decoratin manager until 1922 at the age of 19. Perhaps he followed on wit similar designs which were inspired by the earlier GRECIA pattern, but the general consensus of opinion seems to weigh i favour of Reginald Thompson's talented Aerographing Depar ment devising and implementing these designs during the 1930'

The decoration names are stamped on the base of ware GRECIAN, CHINESE and EGYPTIAN names are boxed cap tals, which may indicate these patterns were earlier than th other decoration names which are written in sloping style.

Similar aerographed multi coloured but more structured pa terns of flowers, and trees e.g. PEONA, WENTWORTH, MAR GUERITE and THE GLEN were also of the same theme, an freehand. The artists responsible for these intricate patter were very highly skilled but during the war many of them we conscripted either for war work or the forces. After the war became difficult to find skilled operatives able to do this wo and most of the patterns ceased. Two patterns which did co tinue were DOVEDALE an embossed flower pattern requirin considerable handpainting skills, and ROSSLYN a slightly easi decoration due to the lithographed flower pattern.

Lustre ware was part of the Thomas Lawrence productio this is often found on FLOSMARON biscuit barrels and honi but also on a few other items, and I have noticed some of th abstract patterns have a lustre finish. The figures, animals, an some novelties were beautifully hand painted in tasteful natur colours. The parrots and toucans, with the appropriate bowl were decorated in abstract patterns or even flowers and cottage The clock sets were decorated in a cross section of styles use at the time of production and include GRECIAN, camel an palm, and the ubiquitous Cornish scene.

◀ Known as WYNNEL jugs, left: decoration 4852, centre: decoration 4521, right: 'Summertime' decoration. Photograph from Anne and John Morgan.

◀ ALLADIN shape 8½″ high, CULSTONE decoration. All photographs from Janice and Terry Waller.

▶ HOLLON No. 3 shape 6¼″ high, KADIS decoration.

222 shape 7″ high, KAVERN coration.

No shape name on the fish vase ½″ high, GRECIAN decoration.

▼ 206 and 220 shapes 6½″ and ″ high, THE GLEN decoration.

▼ ATHENS shape 14″ high, BURMA decoration.

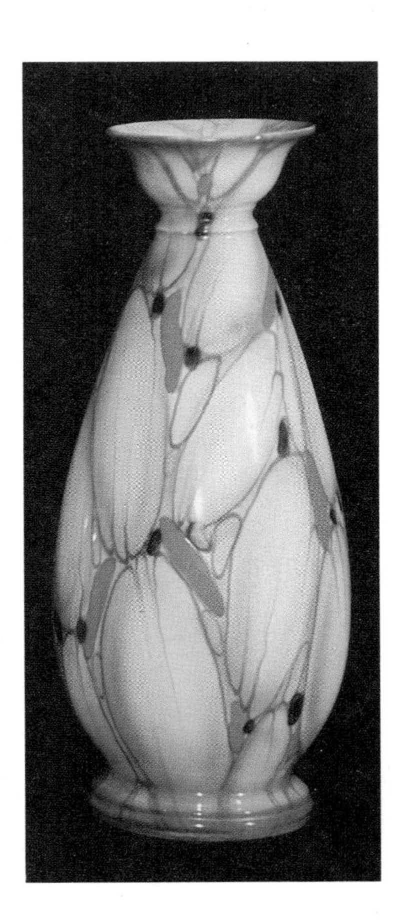

◀ Dishes with specia ridge for holding grapefruit. CHINESE decoration. Also on the base: Prov. Patent No. 4774/33. Photograph from John Paley.

▼ METRO shape 8″ high, ARAGON decoration. Photograph from Janice and Terry Waller.

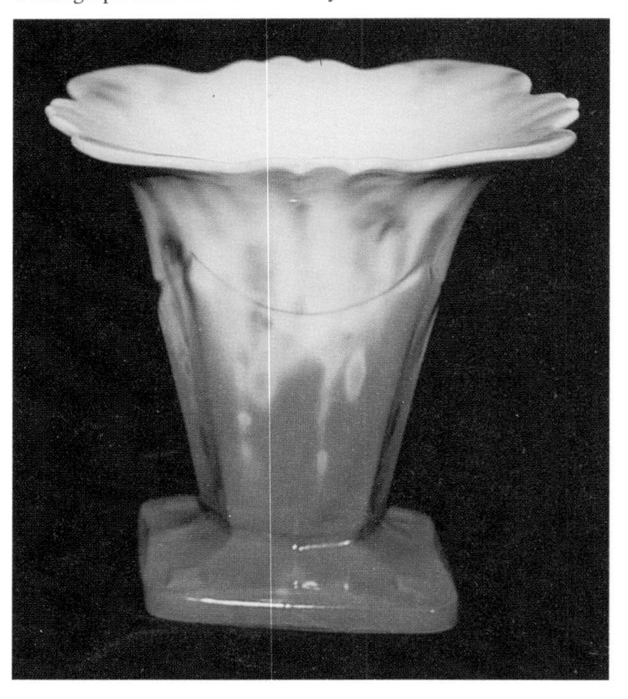

▼ REGAL shape, MELVILLE decoration. Photograph from Penny Teerman.

▼ LOCK and ASCOT F.H. shapes 6¼″ and 8″ high, FLAMAR and GRECIAN decorations. Photograph from Helen Jamieson.

▼ Parrot 9½″ high in SYDNEY bowl, GEORGIA decoration. Photograph from John Stiles.

◀ HENLEY shape 8¾″ high, WENTWORTH decoration. Photograph from Lewis Dunkley.

▶ 192 shape 10½″ high, SHEILA decoration. Photograph from Janice and Terry Waller.

▼ SUDAN shape 5¾″ high, EGYPTIAN decoration. Photograph from Janice and Terry Waller.

PRINCESS shape, PEONA decoration. otograph from Helen Jamieson.

▼ Owl jug Reg. No. 797700 (1934), Heron jug, WOODLAND shape jug, SIAM shape with ASSYRIAN decoration. Photograph from John Stiles.

▲ TOUCAN shape in MELBOURNE bowl, FANTASTIC decoration. Photograph from Janice and Terry Waller.

▲ MARSH jug. Photograph from Sandra Hancock.

◄ Toadstool 3¼″ high 3″ diameter. On base: Falcon Wares (sic) English Make. Photograph from Brian Stalley.

► CITY shape toilet jug 9″ high, decoration 4416, (Indian Tree). Photograph from Anne and John Morgan.

▼ Bowl 3½″ high 8″ diameter with KILLARNEY decoration. Lent by Jackie Kaldenberg.

▼ DOROTHY shape, Reg. No. 773693 (1932), decoration 4817. Photograph from John Stiles.

▲ CASKET shape $4\frac{3}{4}''$ high, Falcon Glendoza Ware (in laurel wreath), decoration 4437. Photograph from Helen Jamieson.

170 shape, decoration 4117, rose bowl, decoration 4118. otograph from John Stiles.

CASKET shape, ADONA decoration, SILVERN shape high, ZEELAND decoration. Photograph from Helen mieson.

ARGYLE 12″ shape, decoration 4593.

▼ CLIFTON No. 2 shape $7\frac{1}{2}''$ high, MASONA No. 2 shape, 5″ high, decoration 4817. Photograph from Helen Jamieson.

▲▶ Decorations 4878 and 5017. Photographs from Marie Hammond.

▼ ADELAIDE shape 5¾″ high, decoration 4912, 'Glorious Devon'. Photograph from Helen Jamieson.

▲ 'Blossom Time' decoration. Photo by Sheila Cox.

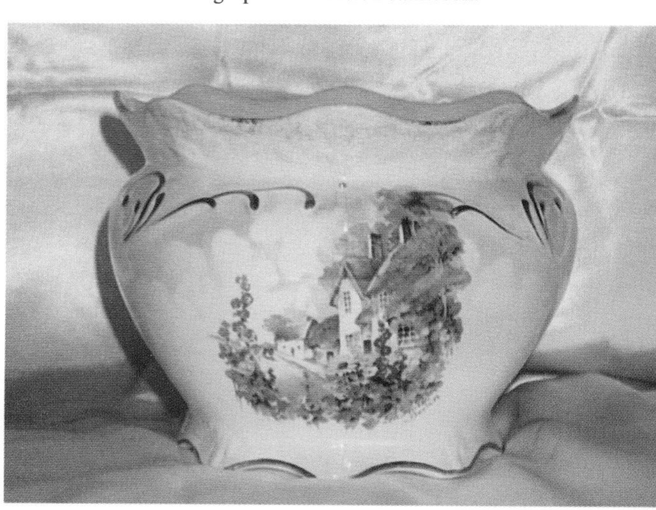

▼ WESTERN shape toilet jug 11″ high, decoration 4852. Photo from Jean Simms.

▼ Vase 10½″ high, ART 8″ shape pot. Photo from Helen Jamieson.

▲ Girl with doll, number 03 6½″ high. Photograph by Mick and Derry Collins.

The Water Carrier (lent by Jeanette Holdcroft), The Bread Winner and Mary, about 8″ high. The names usually written on the base. Photograph by Janice and Terry Waller.

The Orange Seller 4½″ high.

▼ Joan 8¾″ high, Jeanette 10½″ high, the names are sometimes on the base.

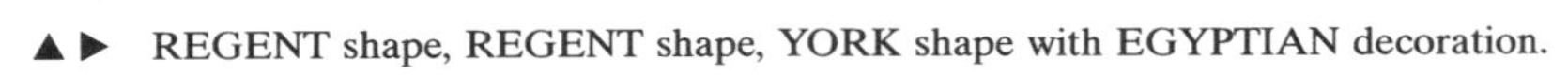

▲ ▶ REGENT shape, REGENT shape, YORK shape with EGYPTIAN decoration.

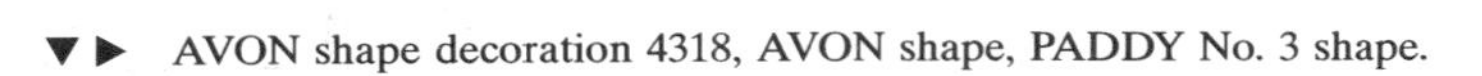

▼ ▶ AVON shape decoration 4318, AVON shape, PADDY No. 3 shape.

▼ ▶ Plate also marked Falcon Ware, STRATFORD shape decoration 4240. 0.

◄ CHESTER shape 5½″ high, decoration 5060, 'The Homestead', STANDARD shape butter dish 3″ high, decoration 4745. Photograph from Sheila Cox.

Butter dish 2¾″ high 5½″ long, decoration 5038, 'Blossom me'.

▼ GLASGOW shape decoration 4869. Photograph from Anne and John Morgan.

BRISTOL shape 4″ high 7½ long, decoration 5147, net'.

▼ Cheese dish 3¾″ high 6½″ long, decoration LU-SAN.

◀ Butter dish, decoration 4716, cheese dish, decoration 5038, 'Blossom Time'. Photograph from Fabienne Daniel and Alan Morris.

▲ CUBAN No. 1 shape 5½″ high, decoration 5147, 'Janet'. Photograph from Anne and John Morgan.

▲ Cheese dish 5″ high 8½″ long, decoration 5029, 'The Tavern' (written in lid). Photograph by John Murfet.

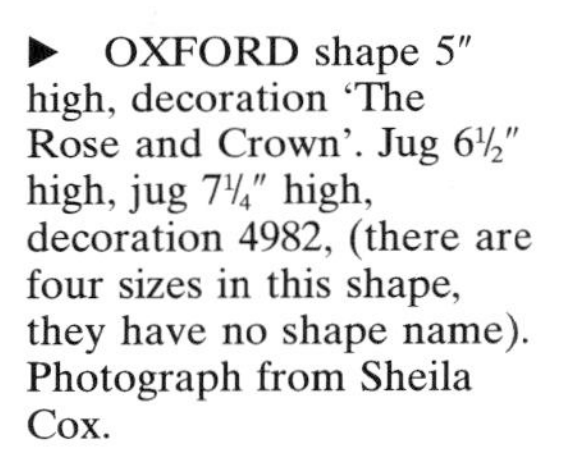

▶ OXFORD shape 5″ high, decoration 'The Rose and Crown'. Jug 6½″ high, jug 7¼″ high, decoration 4982, (there are four sizes in this shape, they have no shape name). Photograph from Sheila Cox.

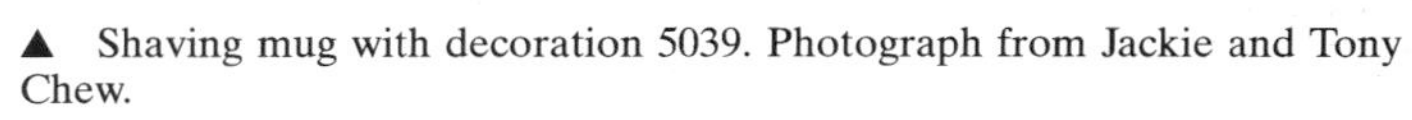

▲ Shaving mug with decoration 5039. Photograph from Jackie and Tony Chew.

◄ ▲ Bread plate with decoration 5104, 'Alton'. Photograph from Anne and John Morgan.

◄ ELITE shape jug, decoration 4991, 'Reflections'. Lent by Brian Stalley.

▼ Bungalow, Chatsworth and Reton ring holders. (The names are not on the base, but they are part of the toilet and trinket sets).

▲ Teddy Ware nursery dish, with the names Jeanette Ruth on the right. It has a special coloured back stamp, which can be seen on the relevant page. Lent by Jeanette Holdcroft.

► Playtime Nursery Ware. Lent by Denise and Paul Tripp.

▲ Teddy Ware, with Jeanette Ruth mark, and Playtime nursery ware. Photograph by Lance Edwards.

◄ Dessert set with decoration 5113, (Lavender Lady). Photograph by Jackie and Tony Chew.

◀ HADDON No. 2 shape 6″ high, 222 shape, decoration 'Glorious Devon'. Photograph Helen Jamieson.

▾ Cheese dish 3″ high 6″ long, decoration 5054G, biscuit jar 6″ high, decoration 4512, cheese ısh $4\frac{1}{2}$″ high 8″ long, 'The Tavern'. Photograph John Murfet.

▼ SIAM shape, decoration 5014, 'The Dell', signed J. Reynolds. Photograph from Janice and Terry Waller.

▾ TUNIS shape 8″ high, ALLADIN shape $8\frac{1}{2}$″ high, decoration UNARIA. (Just inside the Alladin jug is a Falcon Ware label, which is ery rare). Photograph from Helen Jamieson.

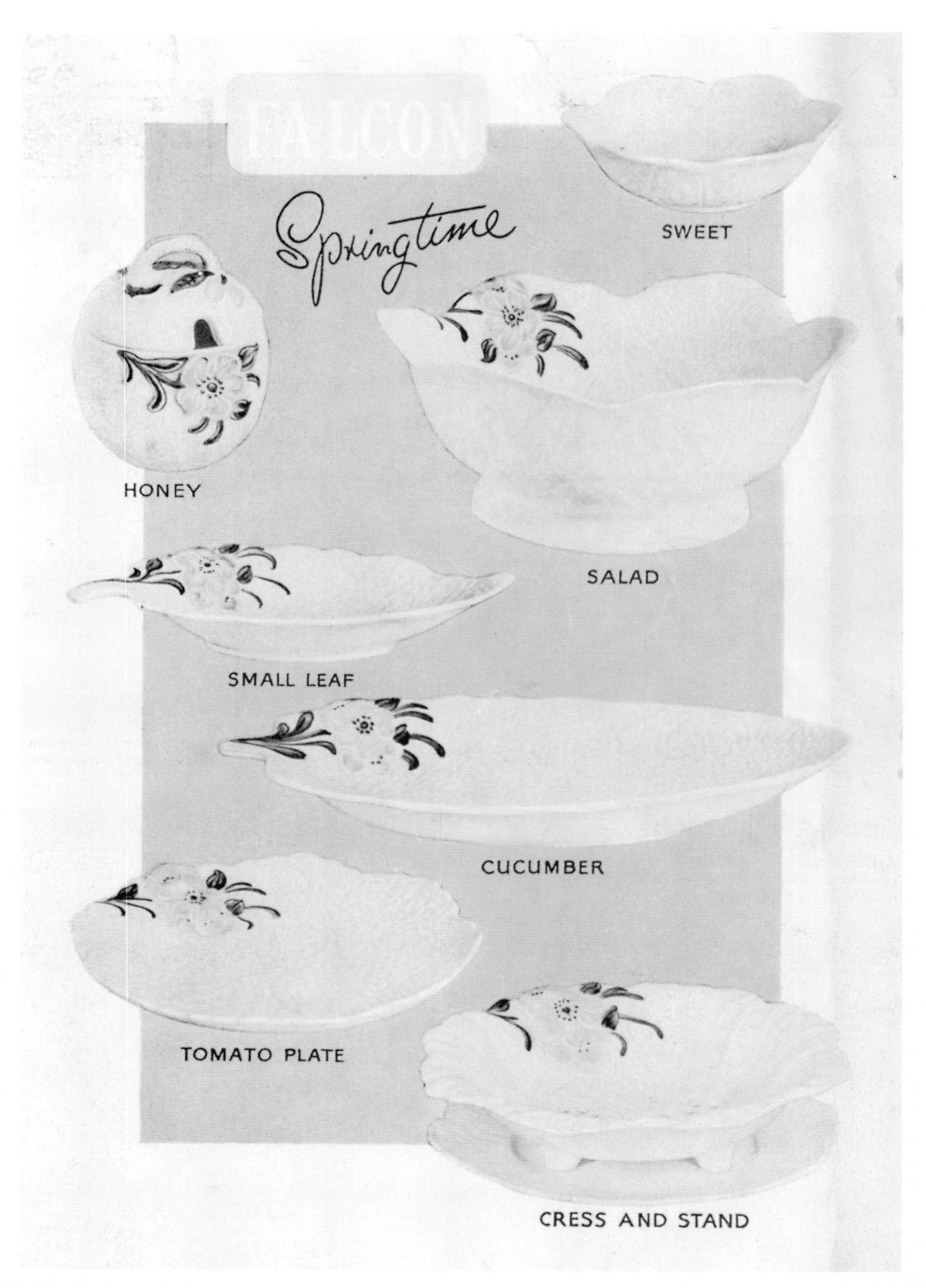

A delightful table ware range, yellow with red flowers or fawn with orange and yellow flowers. Production continued during the 1940's. SPRINGTIME is written on the base of the wares.

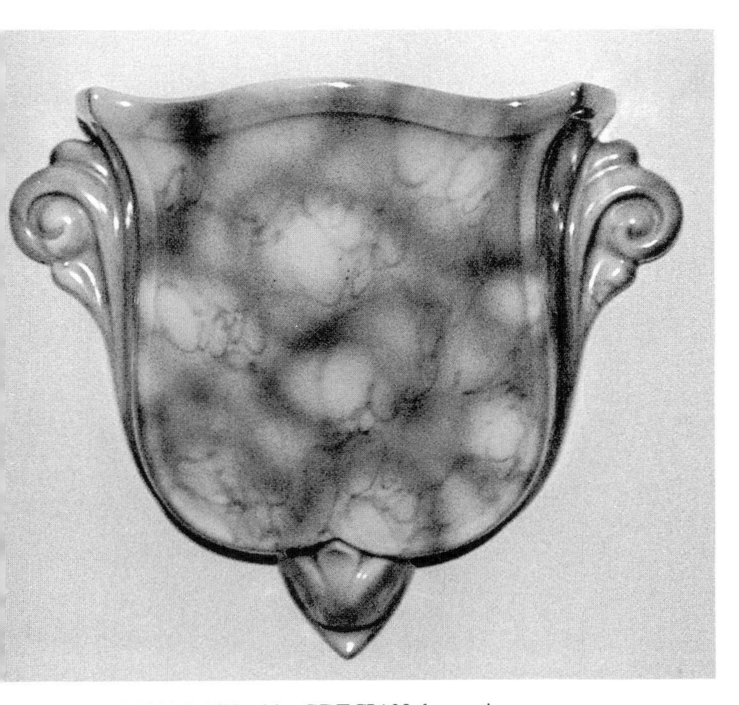

Wall vase 7½″ high 8¾″ wide, GRECIAN decoration.

▲ MASONA No. 2 shape 5″ high, decoration 4453.

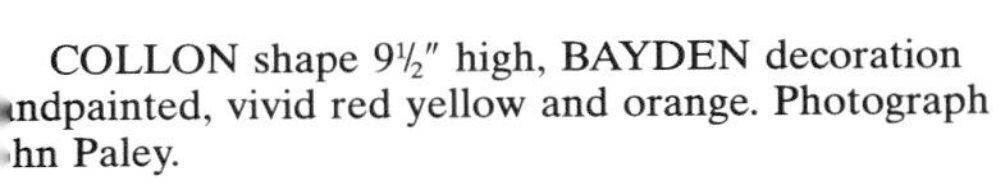

COLLON shape 9½″ high, BAYDEN decoration
ndpainted, vivid red yellow and orange. Photograph
hn Paley.

▼ 234 shape 8″ high, this is an embossed pattern in autumnal colours, very similar to Siam shape. Lent by Denise and Paul Tripp.

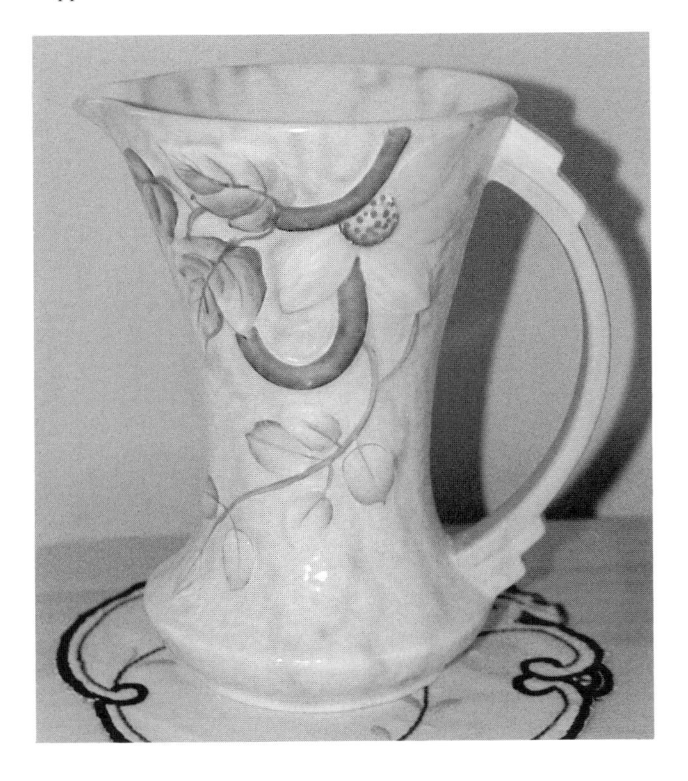

▲ Vase 14½″ high, no shape or decoration name. Photograph from Malcolm Harris.

► HADDON shape 6½″ high, decoration 5146, 'Flower shop'.

▼ Frog on ashtray 5⅛″ diameter. Lent by Jackie Kaldenberg.

▼ CLIFTON shape 7½″ high, decoration 4499. Photograph from Janice and Terry Waller.

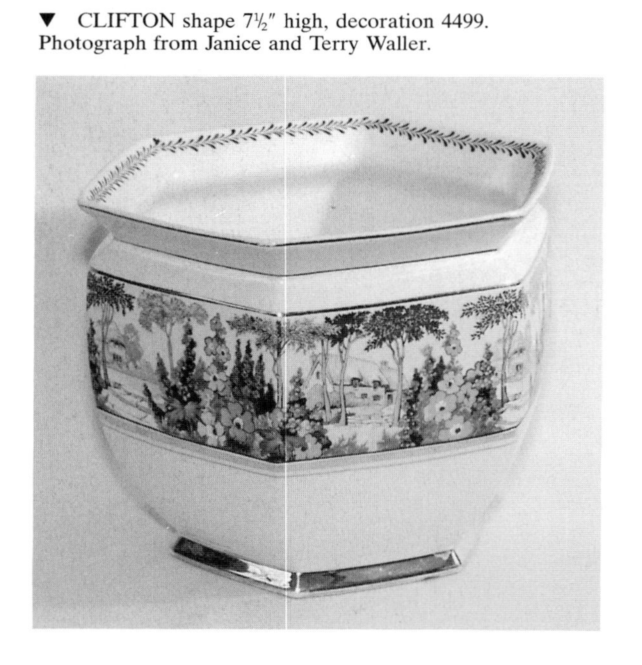

▼ FALCON No. 2 shape 4¾″ high. Pink ground with band of pink dog roses. Photograph from Malcolm Harris.

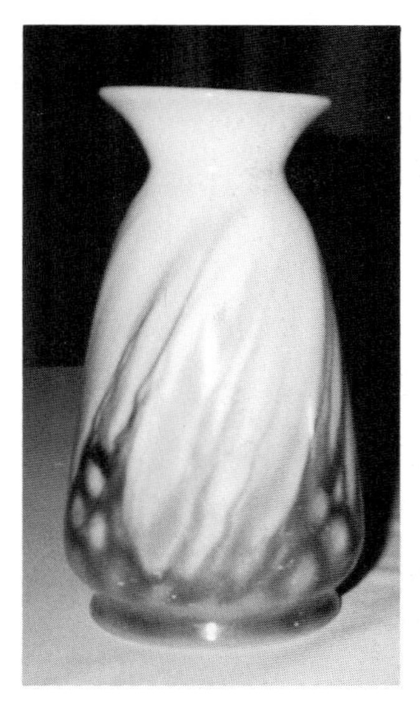

No. 2 on base 4380 decoration, No. 3 on base 9¼″ high, FANTASTIC decoration, ROMAN shape 6¾″ high, FLAMAR decoration, ROMAN
). 1 shape 7¾″ high, 4744 decoration. From H. Jamieson, T. Waller, J. Simms.

◄ No. 2 CLIFTON shape 7″ high, 4659 decoration, CLIFTON shape 10½″ high, 5008 decoration, shades of blue, green and yellow. Vase 185 shape 11¼″ high, 4453 decoration. From J. Stiles and J.R. Hallsworth.

▼ Shape 197 7½″ high, 4727G decoration.

◄ Shape 195, 4550C decoration, from Jean Brookes. Shape 207 6¼″ high, KAVERN decoration. From John Stiles.

▲ 'Binky' 3″ high, from a Falcon Ware brochure.

▶ 'Lady' (the name is on the base) 4¼″ high. From a Falcon Ware brochure.

◀ Leopard 8″ long from the late Reginald Thompson's collection.

▼ Two squirrel bookends 6″ high 6¾″ long. Photograph from Malcolm Harris.

◄ Number 24 kingfisher wall plaque 5½″ wide. (1940's). Courtesy of Portmeirion Potteries.

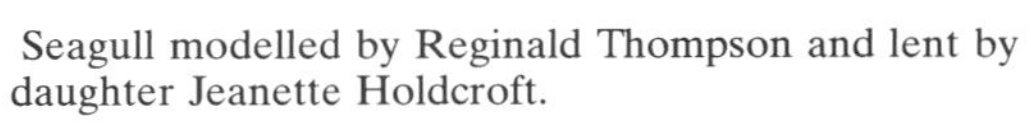

Seagull modelled by Reginald Thompson and lent by daughter Jeanette Holdcroft.

◄ Deer number 01. (1940's). When I found the 01 mould at Portmeirion Potteries, (whilst cataloguing for them), they kindly made one for me.

CHAPTER FIVE

THE FLOSMARON MYSTERY

Was it made at the Thomas Lawrence, Falcon Works, Longton?

No doubt many collectors of Thomas Lawrence, Falcon Ware have picked up pieces marked FLOSMARON having thought at first sight they were Thomas Lawrence's Falcon Ware. Although it cannot be proved they were made at the Falcon Works, these notes explore the similarities between the two types of wares, but leave you to make your own decision having weighed up all the facts put forward.

The FLOSMARON mark can be found on the base of Thomas Lawrence type wares, the name is boxed in with lines exactly the same style as some Falcon Ware decoration names. The words English Make are used, these words can also be found on Thomas Lawrence wares. The colour of the mark is usually gold, black or green, and is formed by a stamp or transfer under the glaze.

The range seems to be confined to tableware such as plates, biscuit barrels, honey/jam pots and various containers, bowls and dredgers. Many of the items have an impressed MADE IN ENGLAND, and shape name on the base in exactly the same style as Falcon Ware. Also hand painted on the base of some pieces of FLOSMARON are decoration numbers, some of which have been found in the Thomas Lawrence pattern book. One biscuit barrel has the EGYPTIAN decoration, the name clearly on the base in the identical boxed in style of Thomas Lawrence. Another has THE DELL on the base, others also have w known Thomas Lawrence patterns.

The FLOSMARON plates are exactly the same size and sh as the Thomas Lawrence plates, and the final and most import piece of evidence was found on the back of a plate which is a stand. The FLOSMARON mark could be clearly seen, part of another mark was hidden under the stand where it fi on to the plate. When this was removed the words FALC WARE were revealed!

Despite all these clues linking FLOSMARON with Thor Lawrence Falcon Ware, no mention of the name has been fou in the pattern book, on any documents or in any paperwo Former employees of the company have no recollection of name, and it has not been found in any books. Judging the pattern numbers used these items were made around late 1920's and early 1930's.

I am 99% certain FLOSMARON was made in the Thor Lawrence Falcon Works, and as the majority of their product was sold through the wholesale trade before the war, it is lik it was a name used by a wholesaler who preferred to sell un his own name. However if anyone can shed any light on intriguing mystery and add another piece to the jigsaw, we all be delighted to know.

A Flosmaron biscuit jar in orange lustre. The decoration number is unreadable, and there is no shape name.

▲ A Flosmaron biscuit jar, no decoration number on the base only the impressed shape name REGENT, which was also used by Thomas Lawrence. Lent by Brian Stalley.

The Flosmaron small honey pot has an unreadable decoration number, it ıld be 538. The biscuit jar has the decoration number 447 which is in the omas Lawrence pattern book. Both have the impressed shape name RATFORD, also used by Thomas Lawrence.

▲ Flosmaron honey pot with the 'Lady and Dovecote' decoration, there is no number on the base but see identical Thomas Lawrence pattern on page 117. The name DEVON is on the base in raised letters. Not a name known to have any Thomas Lawrence connections. Photograph from Brian Stalley.

◄ Flosmaron honey pot and small container, both with the impressed shape name RICHMOND. There are no decoration numbers but both are known Thomas Lawrence patterns, as is the shape name.

A completely different style of Flosmaron, a posy trough, in green matt. No er information on the base.

▼ Flosmaron honey pot, shape name WARWICK, a known Thomas Lawrence name. The delightful decoration of a Dairy Maid outside a cottage has yet to be identified as Thomas Lawrence. Lent by Brian Stalley.

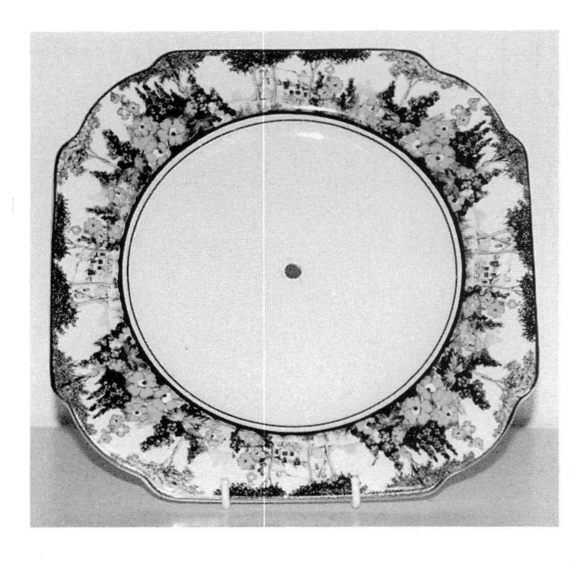

◀ ▶ Two Flosmaron plates, no decoration numbers, but the pattern on the left, can be seen on page 141. The plates are the same shape as Thomas Lawrence plates. Photographs from Brian Stalley.

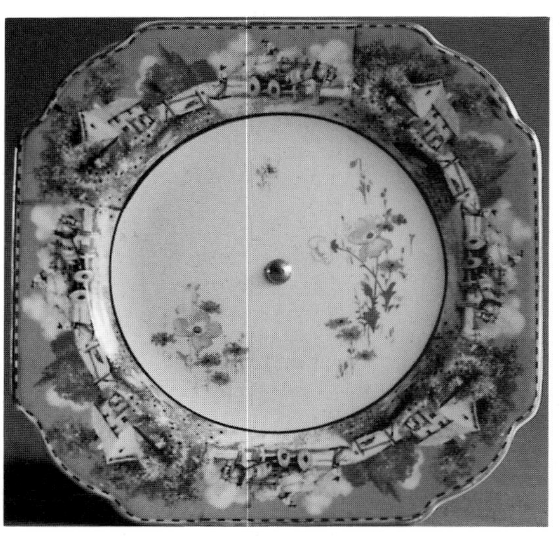

▲ This Flosmaron plate is beautifully decorated with 'The Harvesters' pattern, often used by Thomas Lawrence. Photograph from Anne and John Morgan.

▶ This biscuit jar has the impressed shape name PADDY No. 3 on the base, another Thomas Lawrence shape. The decoration is the same as the plate above left. (See also page 144.) Photograph from Brian Stalley.

◀ A delightful container for sugar lumps, with a well known Thomas Lawrence pattern (see page 126) and impressed shape name AVON. The base of a honey pot with the raised shape name DEVON, and a familiar looking pattern. Both marked Flosmaron.

There are colour photographs of other FLOSMARON pieces on page 136, and samples of the backstamps on page 164.

CHAPTER SIX

LIST OF SHAPE NAMES AND NUMBERS, AND PATTERN NAMES

THOMAS LAWRENCE SHAPE NAMES

npressed or raised shape (or mould) names can be found on ie base of many Thomas Lawrence wares. The following list as been compiled gradually over many years, from various ources. A question mark ? indicates there is some doubt about ie information. N/I means no further information available. lease note the dates are a guide only, due to lack of any definite roduction dates available.

pprox ATE	SHAPE NAME	DESCRIPTION	Illustrated on PAGE
920's	ACME	Rose bowl	
920's	ADELAIDE	Plant pot 5¾″h 7½″dia	134
931	ALADDIN	Flower jug 8½″h	113, 129, 141
936	ALEX No.1	Jug 11½″h	113
936	ALEX No.2	Jug 9½″h	113
920's	ALGIERS	Vase 10″h	112
920's	ALTON	Vase set, centre on pedestal, two side vases 17½″h	111
920's	ARGYLE 12	Vase 12″h	133
920's	ARGYLE 14	Vase 14″h	
930's	ARRON	Bowl	113
920's	ART 6	Plant pot 6″h	
920's	ART 8	Plant pot 8″h	134
920's	ART 9	Plant pot 9″h	
920's	ART 10	Plant pot 10″h	
930's	ASCOT F.H.	Vase with flower holder insert 9″h	114
	ASTOR No.3	Vase? 12″h	
920's	ATHENS	Vase, 14″h	129
934	AVON	Honey, bowl, dredger	
920's	BANGOR	Vase	
930's	BOUQUET	Vase	113
930's	BOWDON	Toilet set	
927	BOWOOD	Toilet and trinket set	117
933	BRISTOL No.1.2.&3	Jugs 6¾″h, 5¾″h, 5″h	
	BRISTOL	Cheese dish 3¾″h 7¼″l	137
933	BRON	Rose bowl 5½″h 4″dia	
933	BUNGALOW	Toilet set, ewer 10¾″h	115, 116, 139
930's	CAIRO	Jug	
930	CAMP	Toilet set	
929	CASKET	Rose bowl 4¾″h	
934	CASKET	Rose bowl embossed with Kingfisher 4¾″h	133
1930's	CHANG No.2	Ginger jar	114
1928	CHATSWORTH	Toilet and trinket set	115, 117, 139
1930's	CHESTER	Teapot 5½″h	137
1933	CITY	Toilet set, vase	132
1937	CLARE	Jug	
1920's	CLAYTON	Clock set, clock 6¼″h, vase 5″h	126
1930's	CLIDE	Bowl	
1928	CLIFTON	Plant pot 7½″h	112, 144
	CLIFTON No.2	Plant pot 7½″h embossed kingfisher	113, 133
	CLIFTON	Vase 10½″h	145
	CLIFTON No.2	Vase, app. 8″h (possibly 1, 3 & 4 vases)	145
1930's	COLLON	Vase 9½″h	114, 143
1920's	CONWAY	Vase set, pedestal centre and two side vases	
1930	CORION	Toilet set	
1922	CORINTH	Toilet and trinket set	
1930's	CRESCENT	Basket	113
1932	CROFT	Toilet set	
1935	CROMER	Rose bowl	
1934	CUBAN No.1.2. &3	Jug set three sizes	138
1930's	DAINTY	Basket 7½″h, also without handle 10¾″l	113
1922	DERBY	Plant pots	
1930's	DOROTHY	Vase, wicker with embossed kingfisher	132
1922	DUTCH	Rose bowl	
1928	DUTCH	Teapots	118, 119
1928	DUTCH	Hot water jug 6″h inc lid	119
1928	DUTCH B. No.2	Jug 5″h (also other sizes)	118, 119, 125
1928	DUTCH 3	Cream jug 2⅜″h	
1912	ELITE	Toilet and trinket set	114
	ELITE	Jug	139
1921	EMPIRE	Toilet and trinket set, biscuit jar, butter and cheese dish	
1930's	EMPRESS	Vase round	113
1930	ESSEX	Clock set three piece	126
1929	ETON	Bowl	
1904	FALCON	Plate	

1933	FALCON	Toilet set, ewer 11″h	118
1929	FALCON No.2	Rose bowl 4¾″h (also No.1)	144
1933	F.H.1.	Vase with ceramic grid	114
1930's	FLORAL	Tray 13″l	
1930's	FLORAL	Butter dish	
1939	GEM	Vase	
1934	GIPSY	N/I	
1921	GLASGOW	Pot, butter dish round	137
1922	GLOBE No.1.2.3	Plant pots 1.2.3, vase	111
1931	GLOBE	Jug	
1934	GRECIAN	(Could refer to pattern)	
1933	GROVEN WARE	Jug	
1926	HADDON	Toilet set	
	HADDON	Biscuit jar 6½″h inc lid	144
	HADDON	Honey pot	
	HADDON No.2	Plant pot 6″h	141
	HADDON	Vase 6″h, 11″h	110
	HADDON No.2	Vase 9¼″h	112
	HADDON No.4	Vase (possibly a size 3)	
1923	HALCYON	Plant pots 1 and 2	
1934	HENDON	Plant pot	
1930's	HENLEY	Vase 8¾″h	131
	HERON	Jug with embossed heron	131
1936	HOLLON No.2.3	Jugs 2.3 6¼″h	113, 129
	HUDSON	Round tray 10½″dia	
1932	LEA	Butter dish	
1930	LEWES	Vase	
1930	LINCOLN	Toilet and toy trinket	
1930's	LOCK	Flower stand 6″h 9½″dia	113
1930	LOMOND	Jug	
1932	LONDON	Clock set, vase	109
1920's	LOUIS	Plant pot	109
1920's	LOUIS 2	Plant pot smaller	
1930's	LUCKNOW	Ginger jar	
1914	MARIE	Jug	
1934	MARSH	Rose bowl	
	MARSH	Jug, embossed marsh marigolds with kingfisher handle?	132
1928	MASONA No.2	Rose bowl 5″h (possibly a No.1)	143
	MASONA No.2	Rose bowl 5″h embossed kingfisher	133
1932	MELBOURNE	Bowl (see page 120)	132
1932	MELBOURNE No.2	Bowl (see page 120)	
1920's	MENAI	Vase	
1930's	METRO	Vase 8″h	114
1930's	MODERN	Bowl	113
	MODERN CRESCENT	Basket 8″h 12″l (sim to CRESCENT)	
	MODERN CRESCENT	As basket but without handle	
	MODERN WICKER	Basket, wicker, embossed kingfisher (sim to CRESCENT) patt.no.4882	
1920's	MONMOUTH	Bowl	
1920's	NAPLES	Vase set, pedestal centre, two side vases	
	OBAN	Jug set three sizes 5″, 6″, 6½″	116
1920's	OLYMPIA	Vase	
1931	OREON	Flower jug	113
1909	OXFORD	Toilet set and plant pot	
	OXFORD	Jug 5″h	138
1930's	PADDY No.3	Biscuit jar	
1914	PARIS	Ewer	
	PARIS	Teapot	119
	PARIS	Coffee pot 7″h inc lid	119
1920's	PERTH	Vase	
1921	PREMIER	Pot	
1930's	PRINCESS	Vase	114, 131
1930's	QUEEN	Vase	114
1926	QUEEN ANNE	Toilet set	
1930's	REGAL No.1.2	Round vases 1.2	113, 114
1934	REGENT	Honey, salads, biscuit jar	
1921	RETON	Toilet and trinket set	115, 139
1930's	RICHMOND	Honey pot and bowl	
1930's	RIGA	Flower jug	114
1922	ROMAN	Plant pot	
	ROMAN	Vase 6½″h, 9½″h	145
	ROMAN No.1	Vase 7¾″h	145
	ROMAN No.2.4	Vases 2.4	
1920's	ROYAL	Bowl	
1928	RUTLAND	Nursery ware	
1930	RUTLAND	Toilet set	
1938	RYDER	Bowl	113
1930's	SEVILLE	Vase	114
1930's	SEVILLE COMB	Vase with ceramic grid	114
1907	SHELL	Toilet set, cheese dish	
1936	SIAM	Flower jug	113, 131, 14
	SILVERN	Jug 7″h	133
1914	SIRDAR	Jug	
1930's	STANDARD	Butter dish 3″h	
1924	STRATFORD	Bowl 1 and 2	
1930	SUDAN F.H.	Plant pot with ceramic grid 5¾″h	113, 131
1928	SYDNEY	Bowl (goes with parrot)	113
1932	TANK	Jug	
1935	TAYLORS	Vase	
1920's	TOKIO	Plant pot 8″h	111
	TOKIO	Vase	
1927	TORONTO	Jug	
1932?	TOUCAN	Toucan 6½″ 7½″ 9¾″ (see page 120 regarding date)	122, 132
1927	TOWER	Toilet set	116, 117
	TRENT	Jug with kingfisher	

		handle, embossed? leaves 7–8"h	
33	TUDOR	Toilet set	
	TUDOR No.1	Jug 7½"h	
	TUDOR No.2	Jug 7"h	
	TUDOR No.3	Jug	
30's	TULIP	Vase	
35	TUNIS	Flower jug	114, 141
30's	TYNE	Flower jug	114
30	UNIVERSAL	Bowl	
	UNIVERSAL No.3	Jug 5¾"h (also probably 1 & 2)	
34	VICTOR	Toilet set	115, 117
30's	WARWICK	Honey pot	
32	WESTERN	Toilet set, jug 11"h	134
	WESTERN	Vase with ceramic grid	
30's	WHITLEY	Jug and vase	114
23	WINCHESTER	Toilet set	
32	WINDSOR	Rose bowl 6½"h 10½" wide	112
30's	WOODLAND	Butterfly jug 7"h	131
30	WYNNEL	Jug 6⅜"h	128
28	YORK	Toilet set, pot, vase, biscuit jar	

SHAPE NUMBERS

e following early shape numbers have been taken from the ttern Book, occasionally there has been a sketch of the shape, ierwise there is no description.

TE	SHAPE NUMBER	DESCRIPTION
00	1	N/I
00	12	N/I
00	13	N/I
04	20	N/I
05	21	Jug
06	22	N/I
06	23	Ewer
07	25	N/I
07	30	N/I
07	32	Jug
07	33	Jug
09	36	N/I
09	37	Toilet set
12	40	N/I

elow are some of the pre-war numbers of the Thomas Law- nce company, some of the products were used for many years Shaw & Copestake. A new numbering system was started 940 from number 1 to 759, consequently it has been difficult determine which vases and jugs were the originals. I have refully studied the 1939 photograph taken at the British Indus- ies Fair of the Thomas Lawrence stand, and can find no prod- ts numbers beyond 245. This leads me to believe the 'new' mbering system may have started around that date. A list of ew' numbers can be found in The SylvaC Story.

ie Thomas Lawrence company continued using number 37 and shapes until at least 1924. I cannot account for the consider- ble gap in the numbers, and cannot be sure of the date of umber 120, but have worked back from a known date of 1931 d 1933.

DATE	SHAPE NUMBER	DESCRIPTION	Illustrated on PAGE
1924	120	Vase	110
1924	126	Vase	
1925	170	Vase 14½"h	133
1925	181	Vase	
1925	182	Vase	
1926	183	Vase	
1926	184	Vase 14"h embossed (two styles)	110
1927	185	Vase 11¼"h	145
1927	186	Vase	
1928	187	Vase	
1928	188	Vase 12"h	
1929	192	Vase	114, 131
1930	193	Vase 10½"h	
1930	195	Vase 7½"h	145
1931–82	196	Vase 7½"h	
1931–82	196	Ginger jar 9½"h	
1931	197	Vase 7½"h	145
	197	Ginger jar 10¼"h	
1931	198	Vase	
1931	200	Vase	
	206	Vase 6½"h	113, 129
1931	207	Vase 6¼"h	145
1933	211	Vase	
1933	212	Vase	
1933	213	Vase low	
1933	214	Jug	
1934	215	Vase 15"h	112, 113
1934	216	Jug 5½"h sim to 222	114
1934	217	Jug s/s	113
1935	218	Jug 5"h	113
1935	220	Vase 9½"h	113, 129
1935–65	221	Vase 15"h	114
1935–70	222	Jug 7–7½"h sim to 216	114, 129, 141
1935–82	223	Vase 7½"h	113
	224	Vase sim to 226/228	
1936–60s	225	Vase 6½"h	114
1936–70	226	Vase 6½"h sim to 228	113, 114
1936	228	Vase l/s sim to 226 7¾"h	114
1936	230	Vase	114
1937	233	Vase	114
1937	234	Flower jug 8"h embossed leaves	143
1937–70	236	Vase 8"h	114
1937	237	Vase 7"h	114
1938	238	Vase	114
1938	239	Vase 8"h	114
1939	240	Vase 5⅛"h	114
1939–60	245	Jug 3½"h sim to 222/216	
1940–60	246	Vase	
1940–82	249	Jug 6¾"h	
1940–70	252	Bowl 12"dia Mandarin	
1940–60	253	Bowl 10"dia Thorpe	

PATTERN OR DECORATION NAMES

Pattern (or decoration) names can be found on the base of wares, stamped under the glaze. Some figures and dogs also have the names written on the base, and these are included in this column. Cheese and butter dishes sometimes have the Falcon Ware stamp, decoration name or number under the lid. The following names have been seen on wares, but no doubt there are many others yet to be found.

NAME	DESCRIPTION	PAGE
ADONA	Yellow flowers on black ground (patt.no. 4474)	133
ARAGON	Orange rising from base	130
ASSYRIAN	Abstract	131
BAYDEN	Orange/red tulip	143
BUBBLES	Coloured bubbles rising from a black base	
BINKY	On mongrel dog	146
BURMA	Abstract	129
CAVALIER	The laughing Cavalier	
CHINESE	Abstract	130
CULSTONE	Abstract	129
DOVEDALE	Embossed flowers	
EGYPTIAN	Abstract	131, 136
FANTASTIC	Butterflies multi-coloured on cream ground (patt.no. 4891)	132, 145
FLAMAR	Flames multi-coloured	130
GALA	Abstract	
GEORGIA	Abstract	130
GLENDON	Blue flowers green leaves	
GLENDOZA	Kingfisher and leaves embossed, pond and waterlily on black ground	110, 133
GLORIOUS DEVON	Thatched cottages and hollyhocks (patt.nos. 4911, 4920, 4923, 4925 etc.)	134, 141
GRECIAN	Abstract	129, 130, 143
ITALIAN	Abstract	
JEANETTE	Figure 10½"h	106, 134
JOAN	Figure as above 8½"h	134
KADIS	Abstract	129
KAVERN	Abstract (patt.no. 4917)	129, 145
KILLARNEY	Flowers, pastel colours	132
LADY	On spaniel dog	146
LAHORE	Large yellow flower	
LUNARIA	Leaves on fawn ground	141
LU-SAN	Chinese flowers	137
MARLBOROUGH	Flowers	
MARGUERITE	Pink and blue flowers	
MARY	Figure 'A fair and happy milk-maid'	134
MAYTIME	Trees in Maytime	
MELVILLE	Yellow apples at base with multi coloured streaks	130
MISTY MORN	Wild ducks over water, late 1940's. Blue ground, re-introduced by S & C 1970's	
PEONA	Flowers, orange	131
POPPYLAND	Orange poppies	
PRISCILLA	Figure, girl in crinoline and bonnet	123
ROSSLYN	Leaves and berries	
SHANSI	Chinese pattern with symbol for Good Luck.	
SHEILA	Blue and yellow flowers	131
SPRINGTIME	Embossed leaf and flowers	142
THE BREAD WINNER	Figure	134
THE DELL	Colourful anemones on white ground signed J. Reynolds. (patt.no. 5014)	141
THE DELL	Colourful anemones on black ground signed J. Reynolds	
THE GLEN	Trees in a mist	129
THE HARVESTERS	Hay cart. (patt.nos. 4849, 4895, 5009)	
THE TAVERN	Two horses outside Inn	138, 141
THE WISHING WELL	Embossed tableware	
WENTWORTH	Large flowers, fruit, orange and blue	131
ZEELAND	Dutch figures in cobbled street on black ground (patt.no. 4318)	112, 133

Pattern names also appear on the front of some wares and a part of the lithograph.

NAME	DESCRIPTION	PAGE
A BIT OF OLD ENGLAND	Thatched cottage with garden. (patt.nos. 4504, 4713, 4729 etc.)	115
ALTON	Steps down hill through garden of flowers. (patt.no. 5104)	116, 139
A MIDSUMMER DAY	Cottage, crazy paving and garden (patt.nos. 5164, 5171, 5188)	
BLOSSOM TIME	Spring flowers, and water lilies	134, 137, 13
BRIDGEMERE	Cottage behind bridge, stream and flowers. (patt.nos. 5122, 5124)	
DICKENS DAYS	Two designs: Coach in motion, Coach standing at Inn	136
DOWN SOMERSET WAY	Village square. (patt.no. 5154)	
ELLESMERE	Tree and cows in water. (patt.nos. 4909, 4927)	
GLORIOUS DEVON	Row of thatched cottages and hollyhocks. (patt.nos. 4902, 4911, 4912, 4920, 4923, 4925, 4938)	134, 141
HOMESTEAD	Thatched cottage (patt.nos. 5060, 5063, 5165)	137

ANET	Romantic couple in garden. (patt.nos. 5147, 5161)	137, 138
ADY JANE	Lady in sedan chair and gentleman on horse. (patt.nos. 4965, 4966, 4967, 5100)	
IARKET DAY	Village market. (patt.nos. 5196, 5197)	
LD KENT ROAD	Coach and horses in motion, passing thatched cottages.	
EFLECTIONS	Reflections in the water (patt.nos. 4991, 4993)	139
UMMERTIME	Cottage with crazy path edged with flowers. (patt.nos. 4686, 4689, 4743, 4747 etc)	128
HE DOVER ROAD	Coach, horses and Inn. (patt.nos. 5054, 5055)	
HE OLD MILL	Mill, wheel and water. (patt.nos. 4685, 4690, 4691, 4693 etc.)	115
HE ROSE & ROWN	Coach and horses emerging through archway of Inn. (patt.no. 5175)	138

ifferent pattern numbers for the same decoration indicates a ariation in the ground colour, or edging. There are probably any other pattern numbers for each design, but the ones noted re the most frequently used.

FLOSMARON

he following names have been found impressed or raised on the base items marked Flosmaron, in the same style as Thomas Lawrence, alcon Ware. Many of the patterns are known Thomas Lawrence atterns.

bbreviations used: T.L. = Thomas Lawrence, S.C. = Shaw & Copestake
N/I = No information, patt. no. = Pattern number

HAPE AME	DESCRIPTION	PATTERN	PAGE
VON	Dredger 5″h	Eastern, (T.L. patt.no.4950) also used by S & C	136
VON	Bowl	4318 Dutch figures	136
VON	Lump sugar bowl 2¼″h	Japanese girl and pagoda (sim to T.L. patt.no.4706) on metal stand	150
ROMER	Dredger	5014 The Dell	
EVON	Honey pot 3¼″h	Lady and Dovecote (T.L. patt.no.5142)	149
EVON	Honey pot 3¼″h	Trees, foxgloves and flowers by water (N/I)	150
ADDY No.3	Biscuit jar 4¾″h	The Tavern (T.L. patt.no.5031)	136
ADDY No.3	Biscuit jar 4¾″h	Garden border (T.L. patt.no.4499)	150
EGENT	Biscuit jar 4¾″h	Band of all over flowers (N/I)	148
EGENT	Biscuit jar 4¾″h	Cornish (T.L. patt.no.4548)	136
EGENT	Bowl 4½″h 7¼″dia	As above	136
ICHMOND	Small container 2″h x 4½″ x 4¾″	Chintz tulip and harebell (T.L. patt.no.4821)	149
RICHMOND	Honey pot 4″h	Reflections (T.L. patt.no.4991)	149
STRATFORD	Bowl	4240 Dickens Days	136
STRATFORD	Honey pot 3¾″h	538 (N/I) yellow lustre, band of trees and flowers	149
STRATFORD	Honey pot 3¾″h	447 Delamere (band of fruit) blown yellow lustre	
STRATFORD	Biscuit jar 5¾″h	As above	149
STRATFORD	Dredger	As above	
STRATFORD	Lump sugar bowl	As above	
WARWICK	Honey pot 4″h 3½″dia	Dairy maid outside cottage	149
WARWICK	Bowl		
WYNTON	Bowl 5¼″dia (no metal rim)	Pimpernel (N/I) orange and yellow flowers	
YORK	Biscuit jar 5¼″h 5½″dia	Egyptian (T.L. abstract pattern).	136

The following have no impressed names.

	Plate (T.L. shape) 8¼″dia for cake stand	Garden border (T.L. patt.no.4510)	150
	Plate (T.L. shape) 8¼″dia with three tier stand	All over flower patt. predominantly blue (N/I)	150
	Plate (T.L. shape) 8¼″dia for cake stand	Lge orange and yellow flowers. Marked FALCON WARE	136
	Plate (T.L. shape) 8¼″dia	'The Harvesters' band round edge, ears of corn and poppies in centre (T.L. patt.no.4849)	150
	Biscuit jar 5½″h to rim	Orange body with 1″ patterned band at rim. Patt.no. unreadable (N/I) Whiter body than usual T.L. products	148
	Posy trough 3″h 8¼″l (no metal rim)	Green matt. Embossed semi-circles of small flowers (N/I)	149

Sightings by collectors at Antique Fairs.

	Biscuit jar	Turquoise lustre with band of gold pagodas N/I
	Honey pot	'The Harvesters' on base (T.L. patt.no.4849)
	Honey pot	Round spray of blue and red flowers, pale green ground
	Bowl (with metal rim)	Decorated with swans
	Plate on stand	Octagonal shape. Outer orange band, then Delamere band and yellow centre

CHAPTER SEVEN

THE THOMAS LAWRENCE PATTERN BOOK AND LIST OF PATTERN/DECORATION NUMBERS

Discovering the original Thomas Lawrence pattern book dating from 1906, was a very exciting moment. The book was rescued from a very damp room, and is in a delicate state, each time it is used it disintegrates a little more. For this reason the book was photocopied, and photographed to keep handling to a minimum. It has proved very difficult to decipher some of the words for various reasons such as illegible handwriting, general wear and tear leading to soiled paper, and colloquial factory terms known to the workers only.

It was considered impractical to transfer all the legible contents to computer for insertion in this book, as it would take several years to complete. After much thought it was decided to copy some interesting sample numbers and show photographs of the original book to give a broad idea of the scope of the information. However, any collector who requires confirmation of a Thomas Lawrence number is welcome to write to the publishers, who will be happy to help. Please enclose a stamped addressed envelope for each enquiry.

The book is judged to have been started c1906 and a heading on the first page reads as follows: 'Feb 18th Toilet numbers from old patt books leading lines only copied'. The first number is 312, the numbers do not follow in order as these are 'leading lines only'. It is not until number 1140 that some order appears, the date on the page is Feb 18th 1906. This ties in rather neatly with the date on the first page, from which we can safely assume all the previous numbers were copied from the old books. doubt some of the early numbers date back to the 1890's.

From number 2099 the numbers jump to 3,000, missing 901 numbers. Sometimes a three figure number appears in middle of the four figures. Some numbers have an additio letter after the number denoting a difference in the colour us The last date in the book is 6th May 1939 at number 5126, book ends at number 5205. Throughout the book there ar number of sketches and examples of patterns. The names the litho manufacturers appear frequently, (e.g. Malkin, Eve Warwick, Rataud, Edwards, Wolfrau & Hauptman, Dav Ryle & Staub, Cappers and Butchers). You will notice the lit had their own names and numbers, and these are often refer to. The suppliers of colours are also mentioned, Harrisons Emery being the most frequent, it is sometimes difficult to dis guish these from the shape and range names and numbers. N Laurence or just Laurence is often referred to and it is uncl whether this is a suppliers name or a shape name.

Some FLOSMARON wares have three figure numbers, these appear in the pattern book from the late 1920's, and not the original 1890's numbers. They are shown below in exa the same position as found in the original book. Please bea mind the difficulty in transcribing which may result in so words being incorrect.

A GUIDE TO DATES OF THOMAS LAWRENCE PATTERN NUMBERS WITH EXAMPLES OF ENTRIES DURING THAT TIME

Numbers 312–1140 are possibly pre 18th February 1906.

312	Pink peony. P.D.S.Co. Litho & gold. Line off.
312b	Blue peony 5/-.
783	York roses. Line off. (chromo). 5/½d.
857	Windsor border plate. Brown U/g blue & green leaf. No colour on neck.
900	Kendall peonies. Pink. Stipped in gold. (P.D.S.Co.) 7/-.
1007	Edwards yellow rose litho. To Laurence crimson U/g neck and feet. Stipp in gold 7/9.
1024	Shell toilet. Crimson & rose pink. Spiked in gold 8/6.
1090	Coral blown U/g crimson neck & rose pink. Edwards yellow roses.
1102	Falcon plate U/g blue. Blown blue. Traced & stipp in gold paint 9/6.
1127	Tuton nasturtion stipped in gold 7/-.

Stipp probably means stippled.

Numbers 1141–1610 were used during years 1906–1910.

1141	Blaze (or Beige) & gold 11/6 ptd Carnation T-Cliffe.
1152	Hulme carnations red stipp (or slipp) off 6/9 & 7/-.
1163	21 shape U/g blue bottom. Mona poppy. Paste grasses Emery salmon top. 11/6. 2 fires.
1292	Universal rose to crushed strawberry 9/-. 2 fires
1597	Ryle & Staub rose & forget-me-not litho stipp.

Numbers 1611–2007 were used during years 1910–1914.

1622	Davies purple & yellow pansy. Line off 5/6.
1644	32 Shape Davies orchid. Brown & green bottom. Leaf 12/6.
1651	New pot Oxford & toilet. U/g Yellow pink flowers clem litho.
1793	Ryle & Staub festoon rose. Line off 5/6.

Numbers jump from 1809 to 1900 c1912.

1973	21 Line off Malk rose & ribb & vase of rose 6/6
809A	**(number correct)** Black (or block) 37/ green & pi Yellow & maroon rose Davies.
37/1963	**(number correct)** C... top & free centre pink & maro
1974	Tutin panel of roses. Traced & stipp. 6/6.
1978	21/Swan turquoise band at bottom. Swan above. Fawn 2 fires.

Numbers 2008–2099 were used from January 1914–September 1914.

2023	Elete & Paris. Davies new group (Hadley).
2025	37/Toilet green & pink Davies group rose (Hadley).
809A	**(This number appears again in April 1914)**, it has not b possible to read all the words but ends with: Davis yel and maroon rose.
2041	Elete. Rome rose & extended in paste. Maiden hair f (May 1914).
2072	Trentham rose to fawn & yellow 7/6.
2078	Universal rose pink to panel green 8/-.

At the top of the next page are the words: Sep 1914 WAR.

90 Marie toilet. Devon festoon Chromo.

99 Malkin 4720. Margarite & poppy on Marie & Non Splash. Line off 6/3.

umbers jump to 3000.

umbers 3000–3099 were used between January 1915–July 1921.

00 Ratauds laurel litho (2263) on Sirdar Non Splash. One fire, good litho 7/6.

32 British rose & apple blossom. Green & pink BW.

68 Oriental poppy. Plain litho. Jan/18.

71 Regent rose. Panel green & 37/Shape.

79 Sirdar litho (Malkins Coronet). Lined off.

95 Elete, peacock ground. Exotic bird & paste, (3 fires).

umbers jump to 4000.

umbers 4000–4152 were used from July 1921 to July 1924.

00 Butchers fruit. Bon. & stencil flowers. Done as bon. July 1921.

03 Empire shape. Gordon green. Mayfair (all over). Lined off.

12 Glasgow pot or 37/ Toilet U/g blue & fawn. Cappers rose & snowball. Litho.

13 Empire or Reton. Cornflower. All over. Litho. gilt.

49 Printed in Resist blown black & fired. Cleaned & sand-papered then blown in pink (Harrisons), Lavender (Purple) Harrisons, Yellow green, golden green (Emerys) & yellow, Blythe. Apples shaded pink, grapes shaded purple, leaves green blown all over, and shaded with golden green at bottom of leaf and yellow out the tip of leaf. Purple to be blown strong. Gold finish. 2 fires.

51 Vases, Moonlight, one fire. Hills & ships handpainted blown in water green (Harrisons), and shaded top and bottom in Golden green (Emerys), moon to be wiped out white, gold edge.

68 New Vine flower pot B.D. blown open blue (Blythe), apple green leaves Harrisons (1207), Florance rose litho gilt.

72 Corinth. Dice litho blown (yellow Harrisons). Handle black & edge. One fire.

77 Olympic pot. Purple & black all over poppy in panels yellow wash and black finish. One fire.

98 Winchester. Violet & primrose litho. Gold finish. One fire.

17 Kingfisher. (Worcester.) Litho pasted. Blown. Painted and gilt. Two fires. Elsie.

18 As above only black.

26 Vases etc. New apple. (Chromo Litho) Stencilled blown assorted colours one number for all with colour put on bottom (4126 Blue) etc.

52 Premier pots done with 1594 . . . . . . sax blue. July 1924.

umbers 4153–4279 were used from July 1924 to November 1927.

53 New Japanese figures and new festoon Geisha litho with lanterns & paste etc. Two fires. Black ground blown inside pale water green etc.

53A Festoon with new figure & paste fence.

55 Toilet, trinket, vases etc. White Worcester rose & paste (latest Worcester) Two fires.

69 Fancy goods including Premier pots & toilet. Davies new fruit to yellow lustre. Companion to Persian. Rococco lustre.

77 Solid black with brown bird & apple blossom. Blown pink, paste etc. 2 fires.

89 Dutch Rose bowls etc Chromo blue balcony border blown black 1 fire. No gold.

94 Dragon Fly, black 2 fires.

97 Premier basket of fruit. Powder blue. Stippled & gold.

07 Hitchings blue No. 864 willow litho & gilt. Toilet sets 1 fire.

13 Blackberry litho & gilt on toilet. 1 fire.

71A **(number correct)** 37/ toilet BD green Premier heavy Worcester rose.

4214 Haddon pots etc. Garland rose litho. Blown 2 colours and inside top. Traced & edged in black.

4226 Haddon toilet set. Rose & dice border. Stencilled. Blown solid colours (Initial for colour) W.Bath process. 1 Fire.

452 **(number correct)** Delamere blown Harrisons amber, 1 fire.

4227 Haddon pots, rose & dice border, black check down panels stencilled blown W.Bath. Initial for colour. 1 fire.

4229 Queen Anne toilet litho & gilt 1 fire. Chromo willow with band.

447 **(number correct)** Delamere blown lustre 1 fire.

4234 Toilet sets litho & gilt. 1 fire. Cappers yellow rose & violet.

449 **(number correct)** Tyrone all over cut to bands blown lustre.

4235 Queen Anne toilet Hitchings willow, 1 fire.

4249 Ratauds Bruton Jazz band 4787 blown colours 1 fire (Initial for colour.)

4250 Dickens Day. Litho gilt Cobden. One fire. (Black 4250 I.Blue, gold edge & solid foot.)

4260 Flight of birds. Stencil blown clouds & trees. Finished in light & dark pheasant blue.

4279 Towr Chromo band 5958 (Black Con. Fig band & blossom. Blown orange. Black edge. & cerulian. Block. Nov 28/27.

Numbers 4280–4688 were used from November 1927–December 1932.

4280 Ditto 4279 only Celeden green.

4283 Bruton bird on Tower to yellow black edge. Note yellow handle.

4287 Alderley blue band to any colour (finish etc as 4286). Initial for colour.

467 **(number correct)** Chromo Jap band. Blown lustre.

473 **(number correct)** Davies blue Alderley band. Blown lustre.

471 **(number correct)** Lemon border. Blown to lustre.

4288.0. Winchester T, Lockets fruit blown U.G. olive green top. (H after number denotes holly green). On Toronto jugs only, shaded usual U.G.blue.

4301 Davies cottage border. Litho & gilt.

4309 Chromo blue band with Chinese blossom & bridge to yellow lustre.

4318 Dutch figures to stencilled background ships clouds & cobblestones. Blue top. Myrtle foot. Black edge.

4326 Premier pansy on toilets & trks. Litho & gilt. 1 fire.

4332 Rutland nursery. Chromo Golly. Forget-me-not . . . . . & gold line & finish.

4344 New Grecian Derby border on toilets etc. Gilt. 1 fire.

4358 Worrals spray with bird on York etc. Blown turkish blue.

4365 Swan band. Blown black & Cobden gold finish. 2 fires.

4370 Athena figure. To BD vases & pots.

4376 Lockets Springtime band Cobden. 1 fire.

4380 Hitchings camel & palm. Stencil blown mountains. Sunset colour blown on second fire. French brown foot. Yellow top (blue inside). Gold Edge. (Figure & Palm touched by Elsie).

4382 Sweetpea border & spray on Rutland etc. Cobden. 1 fire.

4384 Springtime to colour. Initial for colour.

4395 Swinging girl to roses for top. Worc. top. Dark brown foot.

4396 Hitchings Moorish scene. Chromo Newland B. round top. Stencilled clouds. Turkish blue. Ground helio, myrtle, orange.

4407 Dragon Fly & blossom black ground. Blossom shaded pink. 2 fires.

4408 Flamingo litho & narrow blue border on York toilet. Gilt 1 fire.

4414 Butchers Dragon 2779 with J. Davies green border 1426. Litho & gilt

543 **(number correct)** Newland Derby. Litho & gilt. Toilets, pot.

4415 Seville border to colour. Tango orange. Daff yellow etc.

4422 Modelled. Kingfisher Dec. On coloured ground. H. jade green. All hand painted. 2 Fires.

4427 Modelle Convent Dec. on Sidney bowls & suitable shapes. Handpainted on black ground.

4444 Bird & lily on egg blue ground. Ext in colour & paste.

4478 Essex clock. Solid black stenc. fruit. 1 fire.

4484 Lincoln toilets & toy trks. Lucerne rose shaded in any colour.

4487 'Old Manor Garden' with border. to gold finish. 4487g to green finish. Potters Litho . . . . .

4501 Embossed fuchsia on black ground but with blue leaves.

4504 Davies 'Bit of Old England' spray on York jugs. Gilt. 1 Fire.

4525 (Marigold) Blown glossy black. Flowers tarred out & painted in.

4532 Sudan. Convent dropper. Cubes & circles in black, red & yellow on pale green ground.

4545 Sandwich set. Apple. Green edge.

4567 Camp & Tower toilet with lantern & wisteria band.

4580 Blythe N.Art spray on teapot sets. Gold finish.

4593 Arabian black. New style. Turk blue droppings. No lant. 2 fires.

4594 Butchers Gretna Green litho & gilt. 1 fire.

4605 Old English figures on terrace band. Solid blue ground. Gold edge. (Litho No. 4609).

4653 Davies poppy on cheeses. G.E.

4664 Balloons. Dec. 1 fire.

4679 Window scene with pot, bird & cage litho & edge in blue.

4688 Camp toilet. Circle B/red. T/blue. Golden orange. Blue line. London Dec/32.

Numbers 4688–4831 were used from December 1932–November 1933.

4689 Summertime litho gilt finish

4690 Old Mill Scene & Bits (No bits 4690A) Blue Edge.

4691 Old Mill Scene shaded yellow top and bottom (no edge).

4692 Glost Ivory. Finish black edge. Top of handle. Black extension foot. Red above. Margery handcraft.

4693 Old Mill shaded & Oak leaf band.

4699 Old Mill Scene & Rataud band see 4697. Water shaded in P. pheasant Blue Band. Gilt. One fire.

4700 As above. See 4696. Brown band.

4701 Marg. Handcraft dahlia sunflower design orange & red on Western toilet.

4702 Highbury bord on toilets blue line & edge. (No gold).

4703 Croft Toilet Hulmes spray blue edge (Rose colour).

4705 Cappers cam. Slight blowing. French B & amber & T B black edge.

4706 Geisha fig slight blowg T. blue clouds. French B foot. Pink top shaded amber.

4707 Old Mill Scene on Bristol jug. Pale pheas clouds & top. Shaded in French brown & amber foot.

4711 Hitchings camel & palm stencil clouds. Heavy blown pheas top amber foot GE.

4712 Black & white dice on gold orange ground lined in black. Pale amber ins toil.

4713 B.O.Eng. on Rut. Clouds, shaded top, P.pheasant, shaded bottom amber, gold edge.

4714 London clock set, Hitchings camel slightly blown, sky & ground. White top. Gilt.

4716 Butchers all over chinz "Gaity" on Chatsworth toilets etc.

4717 'Dorothy' Handcraft (Reg's blown).

4723 Summertime litho. Blown blue top clouds brown ft black E.

4724 B O Eng. Blue clouds. Brown ft. Black E.

4725 Geisha blown blue top on Tank jugs.

4726 Old Mill blown blue clouds brown ft blk E.

4727 Cappers new red cottage & tree litho & red finish

4727A Gold finish.

4728 Eastern camel & temple. Turk.b. clouds, orange ground, (Cappers) slight on Bung. Gilt. (Art pots col.edge blown inside).

4740 Victorian garden scene. (Hitchings) (Dolly Varden). Stencil blown clouds (Longmore blue). Gilt edge. Bung & S.Sets etc.

4741 Victorian Garden S. (Hitchings) (Dolly Varden). As above with Wist border. Blue edge. Rutland & litho pots. 4741G – gold edge. 4741B – blue edge.

4743 Summertime to fern border blown clouds. Gilt Edge.

4746 'Freda' Blown stencil deco (Reg).

4747 Summertime to Ratauds blue band no. 6223 L & G. G.E. (Slight blue cloud) (Amber ft on Sudan only).

4758 Grape fruit holder ivory glaze. Border no. B (Hulmes) Edged in orange. (Falcon ewer lined in bl orange).

4783 Lemonade set, ivory, lake scene, red handle. Lagoon.

4789 Dutch fig. P.Pheasant clouds. Wood brown ground. Slight B.

4790 Boultons EMBOSSED floral spray. Yellow ground wood brown markings. Spray. Blown with black, g Turk.B, maroon. Painted & gilt. Second fire.

4793 Boult. Pansy & dragonfly. Emb. Yellow ground with w brown marking. Flower brown, maroon, Turk.b G.orange, green & black. Painted & gilt. Second fire.

4808 Dutch B jugs etc. Gaity chinz. Cut to band. Blue fir Toilet ware lined blue and oro. Gilt finish. Gobden.

4811 Summertime on West. Turk blue top. Amb foot. Initia colour of top.

4813 Gaiety litho on Tudor toilet. Lined in blue & shaded inside ewer etc.

4814 Paisley all over. Cut to bands. Ordinary Cobden finish

4815 Gaiety. Cut to shapes. Black & blue lined. Yellow insi

4816 Crocus.

4817 Glendoza Ware. Done one fire. NATURE.

4824 Cappers Hunting scene. Litho & Gilt, on jugs.

4832 Basket boat & Dorothy. Kingfisher autumn brown &

4831 Bridge pattern. Capper to iron glaze. Blue finish. Clou Betty's blue. Heath Nov/33.

Numbers 4833–4980 used from November 1933 to approximately 19

4833 Camel & palm. Blue pheasant top, clouds, F.brown f orange ground. (Cask & Mas no edge).

4840 Hulmes harebell & tulips all over. Cut band on Rutl G.E.

4841 Venetion ships, yellow, clouds, wood brown wa H.blown, yellow top, wood brown foot. 1 fire. Gilt edg

4843 Old kingfisher & pink lily litho. Pale Pheas, clouds & wa Tinted with yellow. Blue top, s.green foot, (on Victor to Gold edge.

4844 Lakeside iris. Litho gilt on Bung. Long blue clouds Rutland.

4849 Harvesters band litho gilt.

4853 Silvern printed farm (best style).

4865 Old Mill. Litho gilt, with clouds on Bung etc.

4867 Moonlight Dutch figure. Black. Zeeland. Printed Du fig. on black glossy ground, enam.

4868 Scene of O.country. Litho gilt, no clouds. (colour e initial of colour).

4877 'Dairy maid' to Bung. toil. etc. Long blue clouds. Gro shaded cheap marigold, king, blue finish.

4882 Modern Wicker basket. Edge as Trent jug. Glost yel orange inside, leaves blown green. Elsie enamelled ki fisher.

4886 'Galleon'.

4887 Dorothy basket wicker.

4888 Poppyland.

4891 Fantastic. Butterfly.

4893 Marsh rosebowl. Blue & orange blown ?????, gr shaded foot.

4894 Sheila

4900 Anemone on Vict & Bung, shaded & gilt E. Long b top, sev green feet.

4902 Glorious Devon. Iron glaze, blue finish.

4909 Hitchings scene. Tree, cows etc. on Bung. L & C (Ellesmere) clouds on bung.

4911 Glorious Devon. Jug & toilet. Blue clouds. Wood bro foot.

4913 Blue cornflower & corn. K.blue E. (R & Staub).

4914 Sweet Briar. (R & Staub) Orange E.

4916 'The Haven' on Bung toilets. Litho & gilt.

4917 'Kavern' patt, all blown, 1 fire, black coral & celedon.

4919 'Old Mill' heavy blown, clouds, blue top, green foot edge.

4925 Glorious Dev. Heavy blown. Pink top, amb.foot G.edg

4929 Haven on Bungalow etc. Heavy blown, blue top, gr foot.

1 Indian. Wood brown top foot & traced. Filled in with D.red ???.

6 Autumn leaves on iron glaze, black edge, blk & red ft. lines.

0 Bung. toilet Herona shaded.

1 Kingfisher litho. Blown grass & cloud. Gilt.

2 Kingfisher. Heavy shaded.

4 Blue cornflower on cheeses etc. Litho & G handle.

5 Sweet Briar on cheeses etc. Litho & G. handle.

7 Red windmill. Lith gilt.

9 Red windmill on Cuban jugs etc.

6 Bow toilet blue bord & printed motif.

7 D. Varden on Oreon jugs etc. Iron glaze. Col hdle etc.

9 Cock book end ironglaze foot & tip of tail blown light golden yell.

0 Cock book end iron glaze. Enamelled only.

1 Indians head book end iron glaze. Face & golden orange blown.

2 Sealyham pup. B.E. Nose eyes & ear painted u/glaze. Iron glaze. Finished from oven.

5 Lady Jane on Bung etc. Litho gilt. Turk blue clouds. Amber ground.

6 Lady Jane with band on Rut. etc., Clouds.

8 Ellesmere with band gilt.

8 Western toilet on white The Dell print. Enam in purp, yell & red. Green E. Yell hdle.

9 Bow toilet. Col bands & Indian tree. Print & Enam.

0 Bung toilet. Iron glaze. Print Dell (black). En. Yellow hdle. Green E.

mbers 4981–5086 approximately 1935–1937.

1 Bow toilet col.bands & new flower motif. Enam & gold edge.

5 Woodland band on toilet. Long blue clouds & top, gold edge & foot & line under band.

8 Hitchings new Pink Lady on toilet. B.E. on plates. L & Gilt. 'Day Dreams'. Long Blue Cluuds.

0 Butchers 'Toreador' on white jugs. Gold E.

1 Butchers Reflections. Lakeside scene with swans. Long blue clouds. Gilt.

4 Hitchings corn & poppies. L. Gilt. Cuban jug, col.finish.

6 Dell to Johnson and Mathey's egg blue ground. Flowers blown in pink purple, & g.orange. 2 fires & gilt. Pink inside.

7 Hulmes poppy spray on teapots etc. Red & brown fin. G.E. on Glasgow.

2 Hulmes tulip & fence on Bristol cheeses etc. Green hdle & edge.

6 Cromer Rose Bowl U/g print hydrangea, g.black.

9 Harvesters band to glossy black etc.

0 Dresdon fig on Art Pots, blown blue & grn B.E.

1 Falcon R.B. Un.glaze print. Glossy black ground.

4 New Harlequin Dell on iron glaze. Old en. flowers as 4980 (blue & yellow) new col to dropper, brown base.

6 Hollon jug, Courtier, blue clouds orange foot green & tom red hdle & line orange band inside jug.

9 Hulme's Coronation.

0 Hitchings Coronation.

5 Hulmes blk & pink spray on fruit sets green E.

6 Hitchings crocus litho.

7 Fruit set pink & black leaves, gold E.

9 Chromo Country Inn on jugs. Fruit sets etc. Gold edge, White w, clouds on Bung.

2 Bung. toilet, Butchers Castle & bridge, L & gilt clouds etc.

3 Rutland toilets Reflections & Cappers green sq border.

5 Chats toil. Davies grey all over cut to band. Cobden finish.

8 Chromo reserve lake scene. Blossom tree, long blue clouds, gilt.

9 City toilet crocus litho above yellow col band gold line fern border at neck.

3 Chromo blossom tree with blue border & clouds on Rut. toil.

0 Bung. Toilet apple blossom litho lt green wash down hdle darker grn edge.

5051 Old Arc. fig. to heavy blown toil streaked in Turk blue & pink (Harry) finished in sev??? g???? puff of amb. Gilt edge.

5052 Apple blossom on Western or Bung.??? litho & gilt.

5053 Rose bud litho & gold E. (Mr. Salt).

5054 Dover Road litho & gilt. Bung. toilets etc.

5055 Blown Dover Rd.

5056 Flora O????? heavy red, yellow, green.

5059 Assyrian Deco.

5060 Hitchings Homestead on Bung. toilets, litho & gilt.

5061 Cappers all over patt. border on Floral cheeses.

5062 Cappers all over patt. ware completely covered with patt. pale green finish.

5065 Aragon Dec. Blowing. Boult finishes.

5069 Cromer bowl Shuffle's Victorian rose spray, gold E, iron glaze.

5072 Siam jug embossed (Woollams) Dalhia handle brown red & yellow.

5074 City & Bung. toilet new Butchers pink rose spray ??? litho & gilt.

5076 Clare jug, Butchers Victoria rose, pink handle only litho finish.

5078 Queen Anne, flood in pink, top & bottom in marone pink & bottom line marone pink (No centre).

5086 Shav. mugs F Folks spray.

Numbers 5087–5126 from approximately 1937–May 26th 1939.

5087 Queen Anne toilet uranuim glaze as 5080 but with common orange band

5093 Bung. toilet, red cottage stencil & blue clouds litho & gilt.

5095 Queen Anne toilet pink rose (Butchers) with pink band gold finish.

5100 L. Jane litho to heavy blowing gilt edge.

5101 Cornish shaded on jugs etc. Gilt edge.

5103 D. Varden to Worcester style.

5104 Hitching. Alton Patt. Clouds & gilt, toil etc.

5105 Ryder bowl matt glaze U/g painting. com. seaweed, lilac, green & fawn. Gilt.

5109 Hitchings Alton Litho. To H. blowing.

5110 Davies litho on Empire butters all over patt cut to band.

5111 Davies tree & moon litho & gilt slight way.

5113 Hulmes Lavender Lady, 3596, Bung. toilets & jugs. Litho & gilt.

5114 Queen Anne toilet. F Folks spray, Mexican band.

5119 Shuffs dresdon spray litho & gilt.

5121 Old Kent Rd. on Bung toilets jugs etc. Litho & gilt.

5122 Bridgemere on Bung. toilets jugs etc. Litho & gilt.

5123 Old Kent Rd. Heavy shaded.

5124 Bridgemere. Heavy shaded.

5125 Dresdon fig. on un.glaze (B.D. shapes) gilt.

5126 S & C. Cottage scene. Litho, gilt. (Uran. glaze for B.D. shapes) (May 26th 1939).

Numbers 5127–5205 (end of numbers) from May 1939–cSeptember 1939.

5127 S & C. Cottage, heavy shaded.

5128 S & C. Canal scene, heavy shaded.

5129 S & C. Canal scene, litho gilt, clouds on toil.

5130 F Folks wild rose, blown green trellis gilt.

5130GE Green edge & ??? as gold.

5131 (Reg) Blown green & red plaid.

5132 Davies rose spray litho & gilt.

5138 Hitchings spinning wheel, shaded orange & brown.

5141 Davies Lady & Dove cote, litho & gilt, Bung. toilets col E. Jugs etc. gilt.

5143 Davies Englishmans Fireside litho & gilt.

5146 Flower shop on toilets & jugs. Litho style.

5147 Janet on toilets & jugs etc, litho style.

5148 Blue tits & blossom, litho, gilt, uncol.

5150 Flower shop. Heavy shaded.

5151 Janet. Heavy shaded.

5152 Blue tits & blossom. Heavy shaded.

5153 Quayside, Litho gilt. Bung. toilets jugs etc.

5154 Down Somerset Way. Litho & gilt. Bung. toilets, jugs etc.

5155 Somerset Way. Heavy blown.
5156 Quayside. Heavy shaded.
5157 Coppice. Litho & clouds. Also litho on col. glaze.
5159 Copse. Heavy blown.
5160 Rose & Crown. Litho & gilt, toilets.
5164 Midsummer Day. Litho gilt.
5165 Homestead, shaded fawn & gilt. 2 fires.
5169 Gem vase Dk. Marone panel basket of flowers litho gold handle & trace.
5170 London vase Dk. marone panel. Chromo rose litho spray G hdles & traced.
5171 Midsummer Day. Litho shaded.
5172 New Chromo rose.
5175 Rose & Crown. Shaded as sp. wheel.
5176 Pansy p.point on col glazes.
5177 Dresd spray on col glazes.
5180 Dull black. Syrian.
5186 Pink roses & green fern (S & C) on Taylors vases white & gold handles & traced.
5187 (S & C) Red & yellow rose, litho & gilt.
5188 Midsummer Day. Maroon top & foot. Gold H & traced.
5189 Old Dresdon type scenes, cannot be repeated. Mar top & foot.
5190 (S & C) Pink rose & green fern, Worc. shaded. Ti background, cel. & yellow, gold traced.
5191 Butchers pink rose. Worc. fawn shaded, tinted backgro cel. & yellow. Gold traced.
5192 Dutch figures to blue clouds, gold finish.
5193 Arc fig & dropper S/blown background gold edge & I
5195 Pink rose & blue flower spray litho & G.E.
5196 Market Day to blue clouds, amber foot, heavy shaded
5197 Market day to litho gilt.
5198 Blue & pink spray gold Taylors vases.
5199 Windmill & boat S & C. Blue clouds. G.traced.
5200 Chromo tree & b.berry (no clouds) on Taylors vases.
5201 'Tally Ho' (Taylors vases). Blue clouds G.Trac.
5202 'The Green Man' litho on Taylors vases traced in gold
5203 Midsummer Day, clouds U/G fawn top & foot, gilt. Tay vases.
5204 Moorish window scene, gilt, no blowing. Taylors vases
5205 V.Smithy, on toilets litho & clouds.

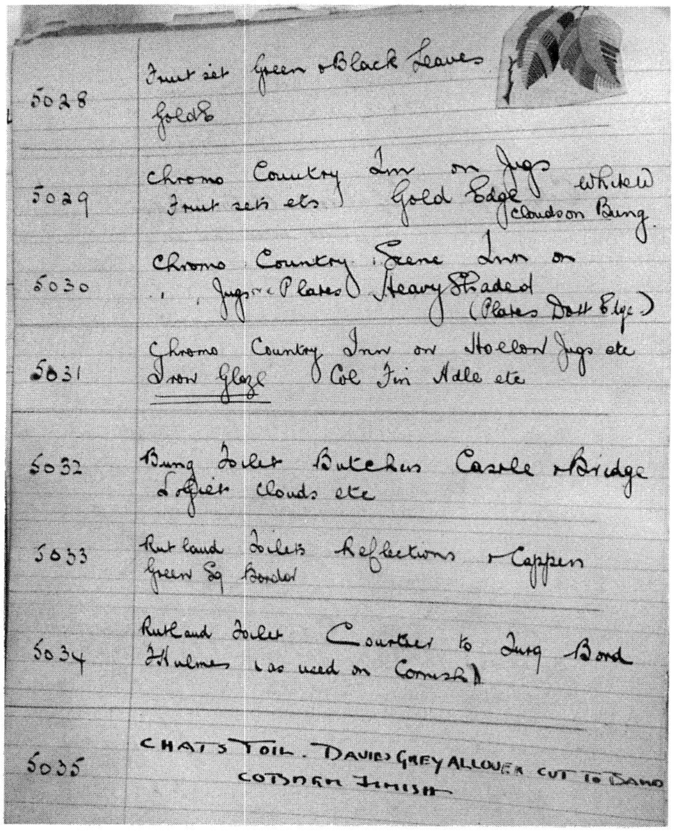
5028 Fruit set Green & Black Leaves Gold E
5029 Chromo Country Inn on Jugs White Fruit sets etc Gold Edge clouds on Bung
5030 Chromo Country Scene Inn on Jugs & Plates Heavy Shaded (Plates Dott Edge)
5031 Chromo Country Inn on Hollon Jugs etc Ivory Glaze Col Fin Hdle etc
5032 Bung Toilet Butchers Castle & Bridge Lo/Gilt Clouds etc
5033 Rutland Toilets Reflections & Coppice Green Sq Border
5034 Rutland Toilet Courtier to Zurg Band Holmes (as used on Cornish)
5035 CHATS TOIL. DAVIES GREY ALLOVER CUT TO BAND COTSDEN FINISH

◀ Page from the Thomas Lawrence Pattern Book dating c1936. Shape names BUNG (for Bungalow), HOLLON, RUTLAND and CHATS (for Chatsworth) can be seen.

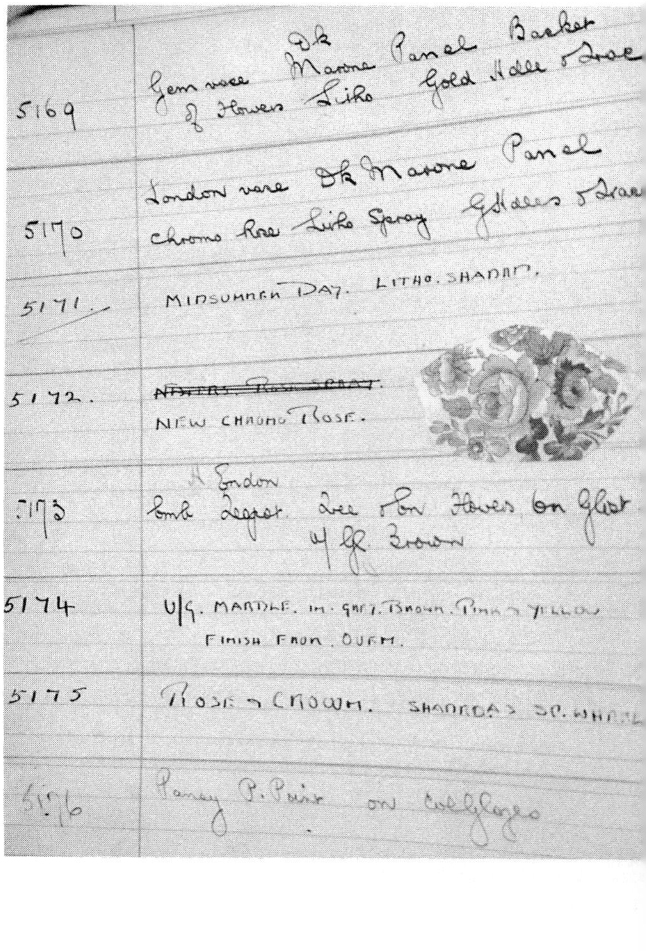
5169 Gem vase Dk Marone Panel Basket of Flowers Litho Gold Hdle & Trac
5170 London vase Dk Marone Panel Chromo Rose Litho Spray G Hdles & Trac
5171 MIDSUMMER DAY. LITHO. SHADED.
5172 NEW CHROMO ROSE.
5173 London [illegible] Flowers on Glost U/G Brown
5174 U/G. MARBLE. IN GREY. BROWN. PINK & YELLOW FINISH FROM OVEN.
5175 ROSE & CROWN. SHADED AS SP. WHEEL
5176 Pansy P.Point on Col glazes

▶ These numbers were used c1938. GEM and LONDON vases are mentioned, and an example is shown of the 'New chromo rose'.

CHAPTER EIGHT

THOMAS LAWRENCE AND FLOSMARON BACKSTAMPS

The decoration name Glendoza is
netimes between FALCON and
RE.

▲ The Banner FALCON WARE is also used without the urn. MADE IN ENGLAND was inside the circle on the earlier wares.

▲ The 'boxed' GRECIAN is the decoration name.

GEORGIA decoration on
ESTERN shape.

▲ A mark similar to this has been seen. (Allow for artistic licence.)

► Unusual dated mark

The pallette mark was not
d very often.

▼ The LG mark was probably introduced after the Lawrence and Grundy partnership in 1920, and is the most frequently seen mark.

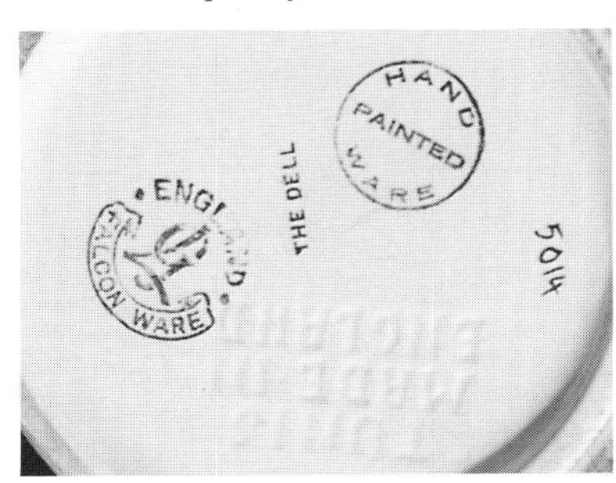

▼ The same as top left minus laurel wreath.

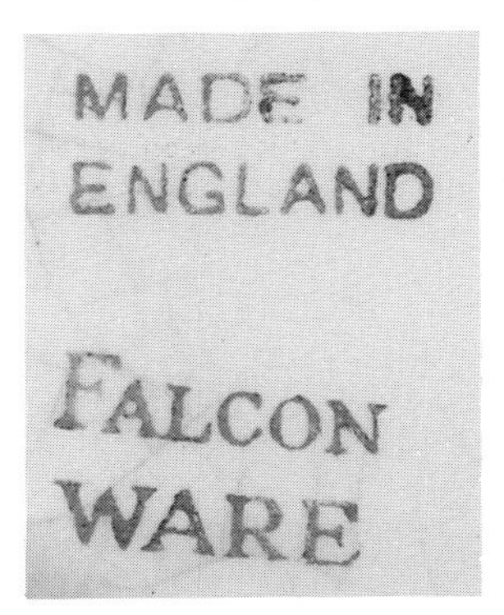

Some examples of back stamps showing decoration names, and impressed shape names. Second row left shows GRECIAN decoration name cross out and FANTASTIC substituted. It is not possible to accurately date any marks but they were all in use before 1939.

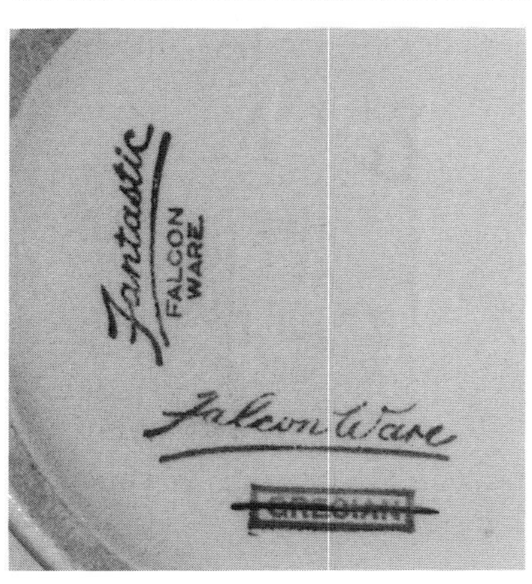

s you can see there were many types of back stamps used over the years. In 1938 Thomas Lawrence became a 'limited' company. The Teddy are mark is the only coloured mark so far seen. Bottom line left is the base of the figure 'The Bread Winner'.

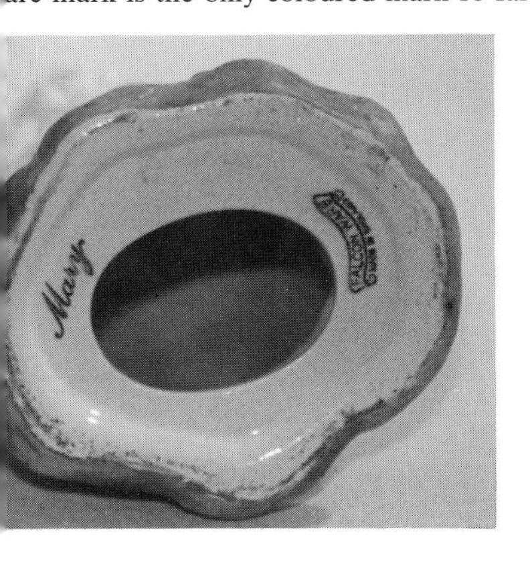

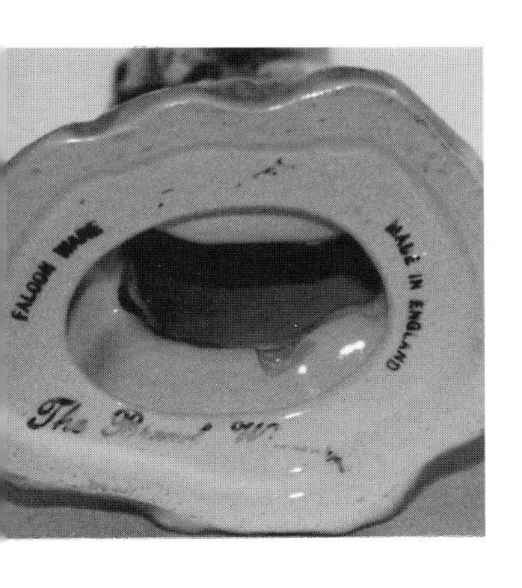

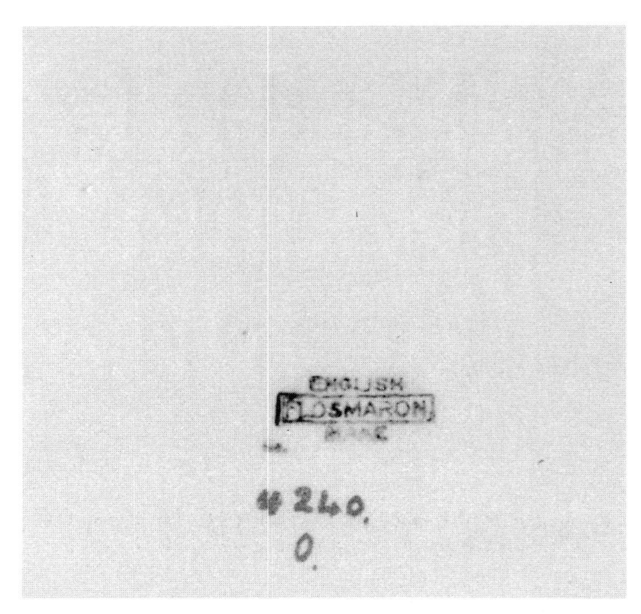

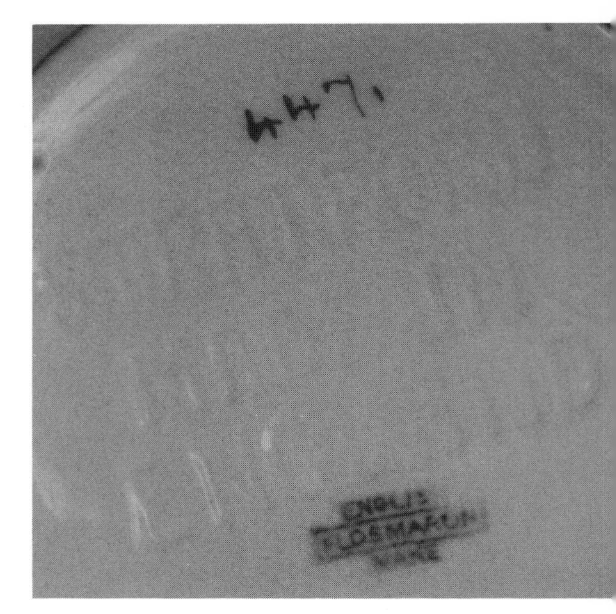

Examples of FLOSMARON marks, with decoration names and numbers, and impressed shape names.

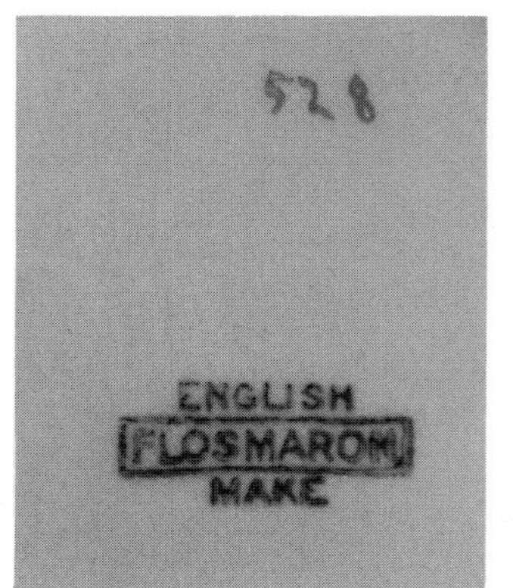

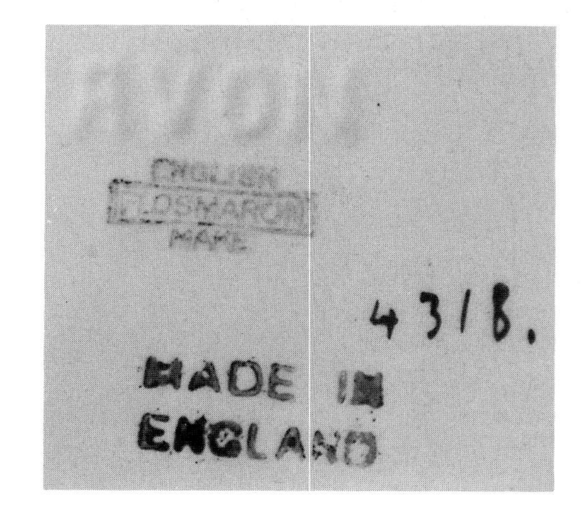

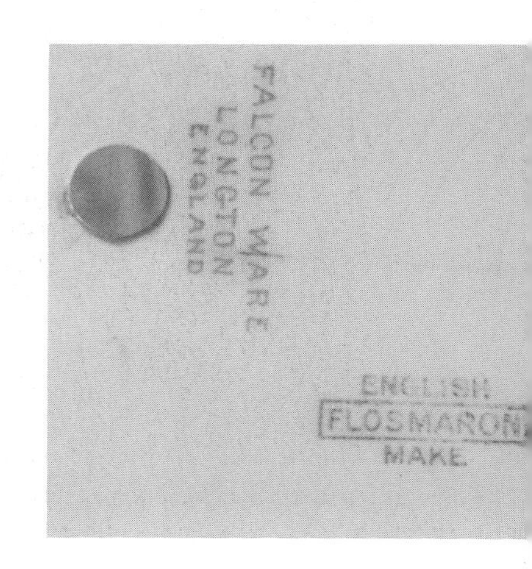

PART THREE

FALCON CHINA LTD.

Heaths Passage,
Warren Street,
Longton,
Stoke-on-Trent,
ST3 1SD.
Telephone & Fax: (01782) 598220

r. Ivan Dean, managing director and Mr. David Dean, production manager of Falcon China Ltd. Photograph taken at the International Trade ir, Birmingham by The Evening Sentinel.

FALCON CHINA LIMITED

FALCON CHINA LTD
Heaths Passage
Warren Street
Longton
Stoke-on-Trent

For part three of The Falcon Story, we have found, tucked away in the back streets of Longton, a small pottery called Falcon China.

Having written about two potteries founded in the last century in the previous chapters, it is reassuring to find new pottery life emerging in Stoke-on-Trent also using the Falcon name. Falcon China have found a little niche in this highly competitive market, becoming specialists in one small area of ornamental china.

Falcon China was founded in 1990 by Mr. Ivan Dean, and is a family run concern. Mr. Dean comes from an accountancy background augmented by experience in buying and selling pottery fancies. During this time he gauged the time was right for starting his own business, filling a small gap in the market. The company specialise in highly decorative fine bone china trinket boxes, in varying shapes and sizes, and have a workforce of 18 who produce nearly 2,000 boxes a week. Mr. Dean has a definite eye for styles and colours and designs many of the decorations himself. The Victoriana range has been the best selling line, but new designs and ranges are constantly being sought. When we visited Mr. Dean at the Falcon China works we were astounded at the diversity of the range of decorations. My favourite was the new Zodiac range trinket boxes, the base is coloured vertical stripes, the top blue with the star sign in the centre, other eye catching decorations were the fashionable tartan designs in red, blue or green, and the flowers, particularly the daffodils. We spent a very happy afternoon surrounded by these delightful little objects.

The range has recently expanded to produce small clocks, beakers, and a miniature toy tea set comprising teacup and saucer, teapot, milk jug, sugar bowl and tray, decorated with nursery rhyme characters. It was a real treat to see the fine bone china tea set, quite a change from the usual plastic indestructib designs usually found in toy shops. Future plans include provi ing matching linen, notelets and other items to form decorati sets. They occasionally decorate special orders of mugs a plates etc., to customers own requirements.

Business has grown to such an extent over the last six yea that the company have already outgrown their original buildin and expanded to nearby premises. About 40% of the trade sold abroad, mainly to the United States of America from whe they have secured a very lucrative order. Future plans inclu opening negotiations in the European market and Mr. De plans a trip to Germany shortly to secure further orders. T United Kingdom trade goes directly to retail shops and depa ment stores, and one of their biggest customers are the Gatwi and Heathrow Duty Free Shops.

They have their own special Falcon back stamp, which co in various designs. The standard mark incorporates the falc bird between the words FALCON and CHINA. The other ba stamps vary according to the decoration on the box, and the include The Arabian Collection, The William Morris Collectic Rural England and Language of Flowers. Some boxes ha 'gold' hinges, and others have slightly raised (applied) anim on the lids.

The factory is situated in an historic part of Longton, Heat Passage, Warren Street. Just behind Heaths Passage is Sh Street a famous old part of Longton, which still retains t original cobbled granite sets, and the old bottle kilns of Ens Works. It is also within walking distance of The Gladstone Po tery Museum.

We were interested to know why Mr. Dean had decided the name Falcon China, and it appears to be connected with love of birds, once he had decided on a bird name, Falcon Chi seemed appropriate. He was surprised to learn there was anoth Falcon Pottery, using the name Falcon Ware.

The trinket boxes, toy tea sets and clocks are of a very fi quality and delightfully decorated, no doubt in future years the will also be valued collectors items!

FLORAL BASKETS

FALCON CHINA LTD.

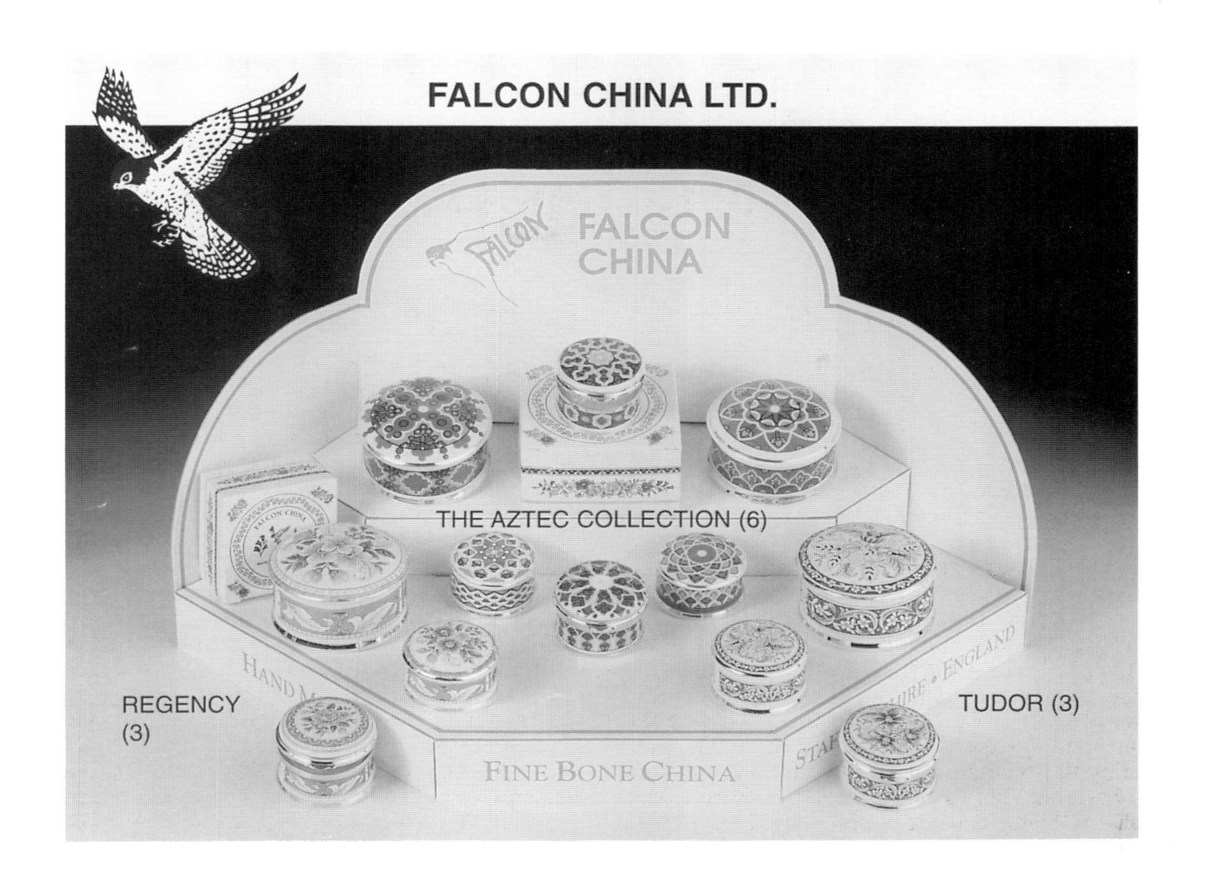

THE AZTEC COLLECTION (6)

REGENCY (3)

TUDOR (3)

THE BRITISH HERITAGE COLLECTION

FALCON CHINA LTD. Heaths Passage, Warren Street, Longton, Stoke-on-Trent, ST3 1SD
Telephone & Fax: (01782) 598220

▼ Sylvia Rowley is gilding Falcon China trinket boxes. She has been with the company since 1990.

PART FOUR

SylvaC PHOTOGRAPH UPDATE FOR SylvaC COLLECTORS

◄ Bowl with embossed yellow and pink flowers, mould number 4949. Photograph from Jackie and Tony Chew.

This is a Falcon Ware jug 6¼″ high, with the later number of 358. It has ıbossed leaves and lines, and is a matt green colour. Lent by Jackie ıldenberg.

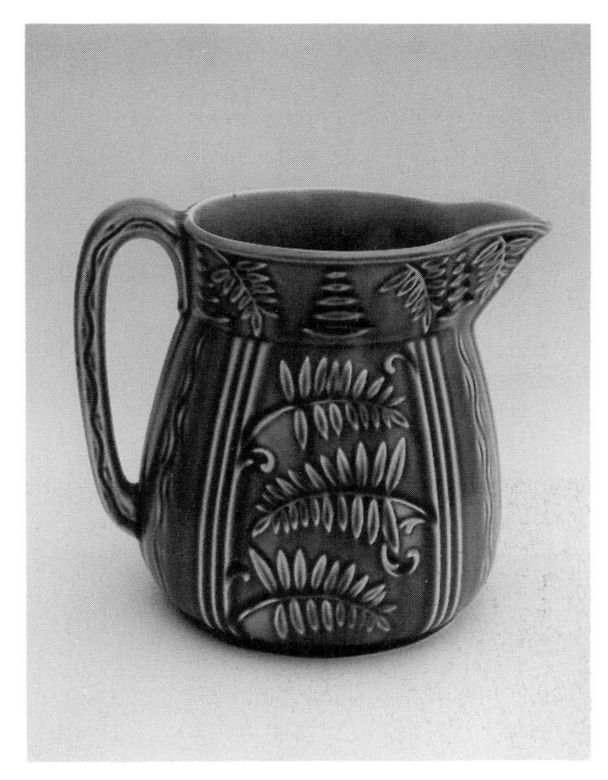

◄ A SylvaC mug 3½″ high, number 1090, decorated for the Silver Jubilee in 1935. Photograph from Jackie and Tony Chew.

▲ This photograph has come from Penny Teerman in Australia. The bowl has embossed flowers and is number 1069, the flower centre is mould number 1068.

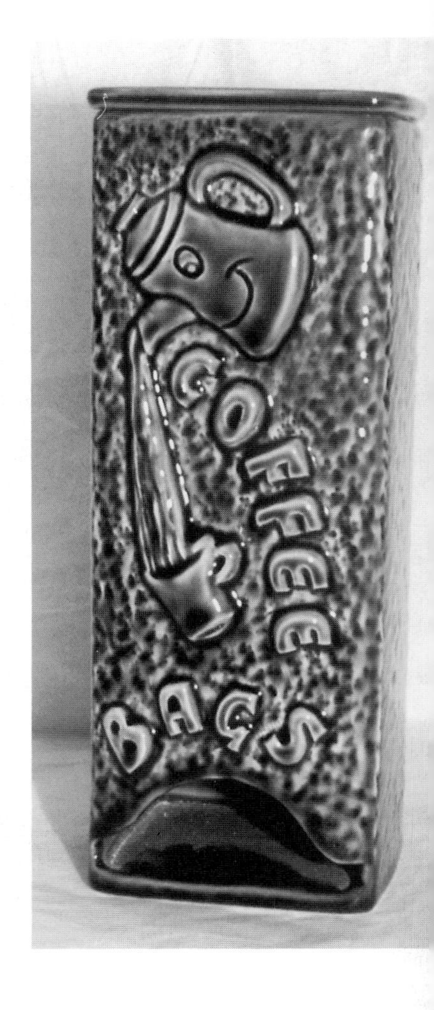

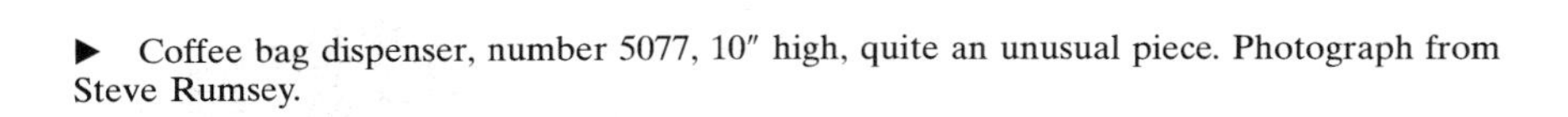

► Coffee bag dispenser, number 5077, 10″ high, quite an unusual piece. Photograph from Steve Rumsey.

▼ A beautiful pink shell with hand coloured flowers, number 2963. Height with flowers $4\frac{1}{2}$″.

▼ Vase number 4864, 6″ high, with embossed flower pattern. Photograph from Steve Rumsey.

Container 4⅛″ high with embossed trees, number 1240, attached a rabbit 6⅛″ high. Photograph from Jean and Peter Howard.

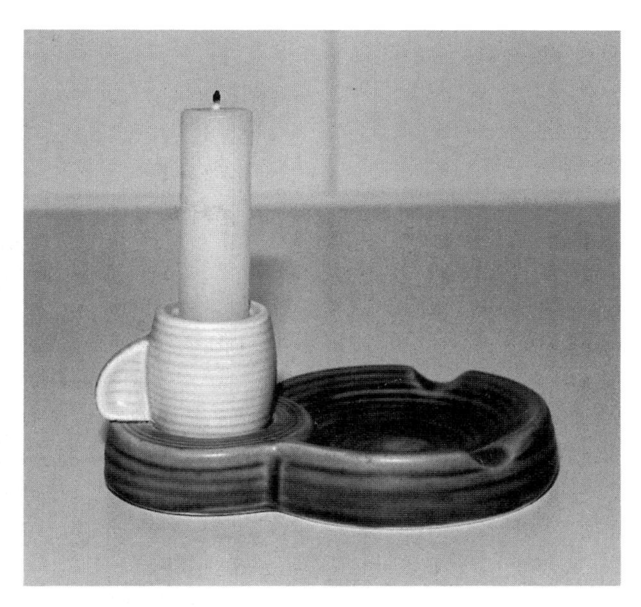

▲ Candle holder ashtray 5¼″ long, number 1482. Photograph from John Paley.

Three monkeys, hear, see, and speak no il, just 2¼″ high and 3″ long, number 984. otograph from Barbara Turner.

▼ An unusual SylvaC candle holder number 1672, in matt green and fawn. Photograph from Penny Morgan.

▼ A wonderful pair of 'big cats', 6″ high 8″ long, in a mustard colour, cellulose finish, number 846. Photograph from Jean and Peter Howard.

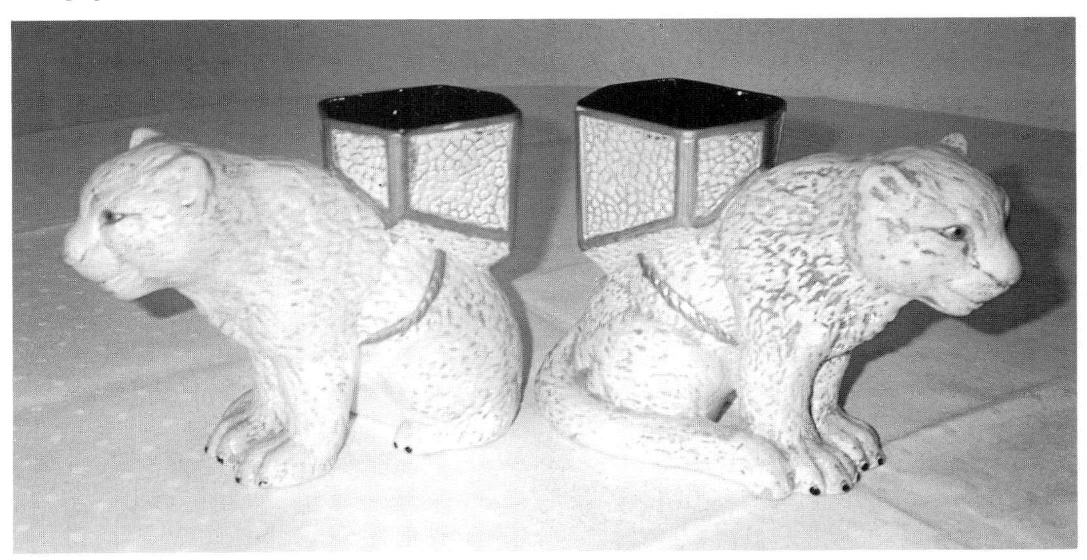

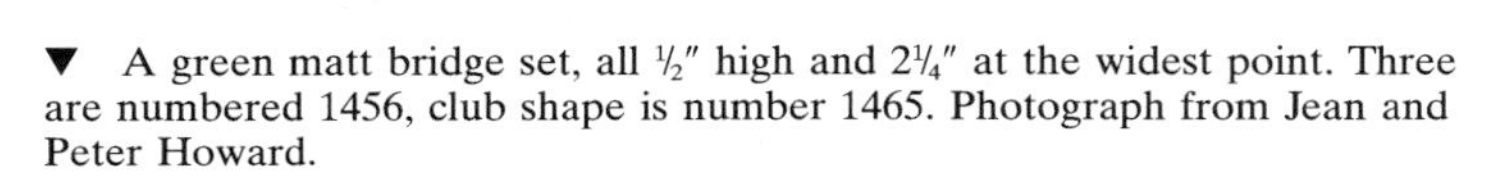

▲ A SylvaC lamp base 8″ high, complete with rabbits, number 1724. Photograph from Jackie and Tony Chew.

▼ A green matt bridge set, all $\frac{1}{2}$″ high and $2\frac{1}{4}$″ at the widest point. Three are numbered 1456, club shape is number 1465. Photograph from Jean and Peter Howard.

▲ A fawn matt holder, $4\frac{3}{4}$″ high 5″ wide, number 2313, with embossed waves and shells. Photograph from Jackie and Tony Chew.

▼ A flower centre designed for a 'float' bowl. It has no number only the old Shaw & Copestake Daisy mark, and has a white lustre finish. Lent by Jayne and David Richards.

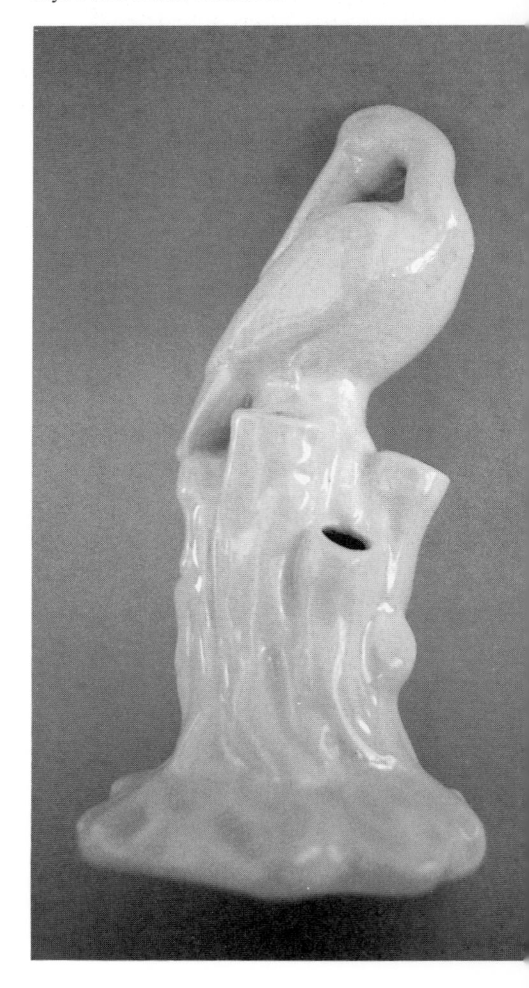

STOP PRESS

LATEST INFORMATION

FLOSMARON

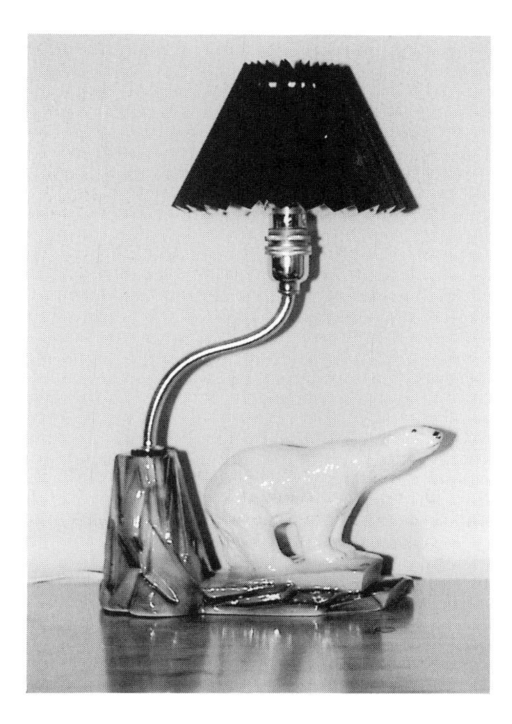

This wonderful bear table lamp has been found and photographed by Jackie and Tony Chew. It is clearly marked FLOSMARON, English Make, in the usual style.

Jackie and Tony Chew also have amongst their collection a Thomas Lawrence, Falcon Ware bear, on the left in this photograph. There can be no doubt the bears are from the same mould.